Everyday Law for Young Citizens

Essential Facts—Exciting Lessons

by
Greta Barclay Lipson, Ed.D.
and
Eric Barclay Lipson, J.D.

illustrated by Susan Kropa

The information in this book describes general principles of law. The legal opinions presented are not intended as advice for individual legal problems. Specific legal questions should always be referred to a practicing attorney.

Cover by Susan Kropa

Copyright © Good Apple, Inc., 1988

ISBN No. 0-86653-447-4

Good Apple, Inc.
Box 299
Carthage, IL 62321-0299

About the Authors

Eric B. Lipson is a practicing attorney. He was formerly Acting Director of The University of Michigan Student Legal Services in Ann Arbor.

Dr. Greta B. Lipson is an Associate Professor of Education who teaches at the University of Michigan-Dearborn. She is the author of nine books for use in the classroom.

Dedication

For Bill
and our splendid sons,
Eric, Mark and Steve
who strive for a more just and
equitable life for all people.

GBL

Acknowledgement

The authors wish to express their special appreciation to two people whose help enhanced the clarity and completeness of this book. Our thanks to Cindy Heenan for her informed editorial assistance. Cindy helped keep us grounded by posing evocative and thoughtful questions as we proceeded. Her competence with legal issues and concepts were of great value.

We also wish to thank Lorene Sterner for her skilled proofreading and common sense. Lorene's unswerving attention to detail helped keep the dreaded typographic error at bay.

Table of Contents

A Word to the Teacher

The authors of *Everyday Law for Young Citizens* realize that most teachers using this book are not lawyers nor are they expected to be.

Rather, *Everyday Law for Young Citizens* is designed to be used by teachers and students as a general guide to legal principles and concepts. One need only read the material in order to lead productive discussions and activities sparked by the cases as succeeding cases build on each other and increase in sophistication.

The benefits of learning law go beyond legal education since the exercises are also designed to improve students' analytical and problem-solving skills. Interested teachers, whether lawyers or not, can use this book to enhance these vital skills which will help students survive and thrive in the uncertain world of tomorrow.

Guide to the Format of the Book

- "Basic Principles of Law" outlines information in question and answer form.

- "Case Study" sets the stage with a realistic scenario.

- "What's Your Opinion?" follows each case and asks for student opinion.

- "The Law Says" provides the legal point of view of the case.

- "What If?" poses variations on the theme calling for more informed student opinion.

- "Activities" suggest optional writing, discussion, and role-play possibilities and spin-offs of the case.

- "Glossary" defines legal words and phrases in the text.

- "Appendix" includes the Preamble to the U.S. Constitution, the Bill of Rights (the first ten amendments) and other selected amendments.

- "Bibliography"

Introduction

Law touches our lives from the day of our birth to the day we die—from birth certificate to death certificate.

Everyday Law for Young Citizens supplies students with the basic principles of law in clear, straightforward language. Most importantly, *Everyday Law for Young Citizens* shows students how to examine legal issues in an analytical way. This approach helps students understand just what our system of justice is all about; how law resolves conflicts; how law balances the rights of the group and the rights of the individual within the group; and how law applies to everyone equally.

Everyday Law for Young Citizens illustrates the importance of law. Without law there would be anarchy. Life would be a jungle with a constant series of day-to-day battles. Such existence is filled with insecurity and fear. Without law there is always the threat that someone bigger and stronger will come along and destroy or steal what we have worked so hard to build. Laws reflect and codify society's beliefs. The development of legal systems has allowed civilization to progress socially and technologically.

Law forms the foundation of civilization and rests on the bedrock premises of justice and fairness. In the United States there is an added requirement for laws. In our country and other democracies, laws are made by the people or by representatives elected by the people. That single fact separates free societies from totalitarian forms of government where kings, dictators or small groups of people make the laws. In the United States, we believe that allowing citizens to make laws in a free and democratic society is the highest and best form of government.

Because democracies rely on the will of the people, there is a special responsibility placed on citizens to participate in that government. To participate effectively, it is incumbent upon citizens to be educated about the issues of the day and about the way their government works. In the words of Thomas Jefferson:

> If a nation expects to be ignorant and free . . .
> It expects what never was and never will be.

The Changing Law

Since people are fallible, the laws they make are often imperfect—especially on the first try. Therefore, laws are changed to better reflect the times. Although it may never be possible to achieve "true and perfect justice" in the United States, our quest for justice requires constant effort.

In our nation, laws change to reflect the progress and problems posed by advances in science, medicine, technology and human needs.* To address this circumstance, *Everyday Law for Young Citizens* focuses on analyzing principles of law which are less variable from jurisdiction to jurisdiction and are less likely to undergo major changes. For that reason, we believe that *Everyday Law for Young Citizens* will be a valuable tool for teachers and students without fear that it will quickly become outdated. The authors hope that this book will contribute to the goal of helping students become responsible and informed citizens.

*Law textbooks and materials have, in the back, paperback supplements called "pocket parts," which indicate changes in the law from year to year. Pocket parts help students and lawyers keep informed of changes.

Opening Discussion

1. Why do you think we need laws?

2. Why are laws important?

3. How do laws lubricate the wheels of society?

4. What would daily life be like without laws?

What Laws Do

- Laws balance the rights of the individuals and the good of the community.

- Laws are designed to apply to everyone equally, no matter what age, race, religion, national origin, sex or income.

- The law establishes the rules of fairness.

- Laws help people resolve conflicts peacefully.

- Laws guarantee that people receive "due process," which means that everyone is entitled to a fair hearing or trial before they are penalized or deprived of freedom, life or property.

- Laws incorporate and express social values and ethics.

- The goal of law is to protect the health, safety, freedom and well-being of all citizens.

Opening Activity

Here is an activity just for the fun of it. If it is true that the law touches everything we do from the moment we are born, let's try to prove that statement. Picture yourself, as a newly born baby, in the center of a diagram with a web of people and events surrounding your arrival. Enumerate the ways in which the law is woven into the fabric of your life from the very first day of your birth.

You may think of the sequence of events from the day of your birth until you come home from the hospital. There are legal processes and documents all along the way. A baby is delivered in a licensed hospital by licensed doctors and nurses. The infant is registered on a legal birth certificate and is a legal citizen of the USA. Mother and child are driven home by a licensed driver who must obey traffic laws. Baby is welcomed home by the licensed family dog who bounds out of the family home or apartment which is owned or rented under a legal contract. Baby is cuddled by a sister or brother who may run an errand for the new family member on a licensed bike to the local drugstore, which is licensed to dispense medicine, with a registered pharmacist on duty . . . .

The list never really ends. We rarely think about how pervasive and important the function of law is in every aspect of our lives.

Basic Principles of Law

Question: What are laws?
Answer: Laws are rules of conduct.

Question: What do laws do?
Answer: Laws maintain order and promote public welfare.

Question: What are the two main branches of law?
Answer: *Criminal law* and *civil law*.

Criminal Law

Question: What is criminal law?
Answer: Criminal law is the branch of law concerned with defining crimes and enforcing criminal laws.

Question: What is a crime?
Answer: A crime is a socially unacceptable or destructive act punishable by a fine and/or imprisonment. Some crimes are even punishable by death.

Question: Who can prosecute a person accused of a crime?
Answer: Only a government prosecutor can prosecute criminal offenses. Although a private person can file a complaint, the prosecutor decides whether or not to prosecute.

Question: What is a *misdemeanor*?
Answer: A misdemeanor is a less serious crime, usually punishable by less than one year in prison (and/or a fine).

Question: What is a *felony*?
Answer: A felony (also known as a "high misdemeanor" in some states) is a more serious crime, punishable by over one year in prison (and/or a fine). The most serious felonies are punishable by death in some states.

Question: If a person charged with a crime claims to be innocent, how is his guilt or innocence decided?
Answer: Innocence or guilt is decided in a legal procedure known as a trial. The accused person has the choice of a trial by a judge or a trial by a jury.

Question: What if a defendant cannot afford an attorney?

Answer: Then the government must appoint and pay for an attorney for the defendant.

Question: How certain must a judge or jury be that the defendant committed the crime before they can find the defendant guilty?

Answer: To convict the defendant, the fact finder (judge or jury) must decide that the defendant is guilty "beyond a reasonable doubt." This is a very high standard of proof, meaning that there must be very little doubt that the accused person is guilty.

Question: Must criminal laws be in writing? If so, why?

Answer: Yes. Criminal laws must be clearly written so that people will know in advance what acts are illegal.

Question: If a person is charged with a crime, does the law presume that that person is innocent or guilty before trial?

Answer: The law presumes that a defendant is *innocent until proven guilty beyond a reasonable doubt.*

Civil Law

Question: What are civil laws?

Answer: Civil laws are the noncriminal rules that define people's civil rights and civil responsibilities and allow them to enforce those rights.

Question: What remedies can civil laws provide if a person's civil rights are violated?

Answer: Courts can order people who violate other people's rights (or who injure other people or breach contracts) to pay *money* to those they injure. Courts can also issue *orders* to force people to live up to their legal responsibilities. Courts can also issue orders called *injunctions* to forbid parties from injuring people in the future.

Question: What *standard of proof* must a plaintiff (the person making the complaint) reach in order to win a lawsuit?

Answer: To win a civil lawsuit, the plaintiff must prove his or her case by a *preponderance of the evidence*. This means that the "scales of justice" must tip in favor of the plaintiff by any amount.

The Differences Between Civil and Criminal Law

Question: What are the four major differences between civil and criminal law?

Answer:
1. Only the government can prosecute criminal cases. But any citizen can file a civil lawsuit in court.
2. The standard of proof necessary to convict a defendant in a criminal case (beyond a reasonable doubt) is much higher than the standard necessary to win a civil suit (a preponderance of the evidence).
3. Criminal defendants do not have to testify at trial if they choose not to (see the Fifth Amendment). Defendants in civil lawsuits may be required to testify.
4. Violations of criminal law can be punished by fines or imprisonment. Violations of civil laws cannot be punished by imprisonment (unless one violates a court order).

Law Making

Question: Who makes the laws in the United States?
Answer: The people make the laws.

Question: How do people make laws?
Answer: Sometimes people vote on laws directly in a vote known as a *referendum*. Usually, laws are proposed and enacted by *representatives* elected by the people to *legislatures*. The sole function of the *legislative branch* of government is to make laws.

Question: What is the name of the legislature of the United States government in Washington, D.C.?

Answer: The *Congress*. The U.S. Congress is *bicameral* (made up of two houses). In the *Senate*, each state is represented by two senators. In the *House of Representatives*, states are represented based on their populations.

Question: Do states have separate legislatures?

Answer: Yes. Every state has a state legislature. Some states have bicameral legislatures. Some states have *unicameral* legislatures (one house).

Question: What is the name of the legislative branch of a town or city government?

Answer: Cities and towns have councils, commissions, or boards.

Law Enforcement

Question: What branch of the government enforces and carries out the law?

Answer: The *executive branch* carries out the laws passed by the people and the legislature.

Question: Who is the *chief executive* of the United States?

Answer: *The President*.

Question: What is the name of the chief executive of a state?

Answer: *The Governor*.

Question: Who is the chief executive of a city or town?

Answer: *The Mayor* is the most common top executive for cities.

Judging the Law

Question: What branch of the government interprets the laws when there is a disagreement whether a law has been broken?

Answer: The *judicial branch* (the courts).

Question: What is the highest court in the United States?

Answer: The highest court in the United States is the *Supreme Court.* Nine *justices* sit on the Supreme Court, headed by the *Chief Justice.*

Discussion Question

Why do you think that the founders of the United States chose to separate the powers of government into three different branches? Wouldn't a single branch be more efficient? The English statesman, Lord Acton, once wrote that "Power tends to corrupt, and absolute power corrupts absolutely." Do you think this philosophy had some influence on the founders of the U.S.?

Constitutional Law

Question: What is the Constitution of the United States?

Answer: The Constitution is the supreme law of the United States. It is the blueprint for the government. It was written in 1787.

Question: What does the Constitution do?

Answer: The Constitution establishes the form of our government. It creates the different branches of the government and defines their powers. It guarantees the rights of people.

Question: What form of government does our Constitution create?

Answer: First of all our constitutional government is a democracy. That means that all of the power of the government comes from the people. Second, it is a *Federal Republic*, dividing governmental power between the central government in Washington, D.C., and the individual state governments.

Question: What type of democracy is created by the Constitution?

Answer: A representative democracy. This means that the people elect representatives whose opinions agree with theirs.

Question: If a law or a rule or an act by an official violates the Constitution, what word describes that violation?

Answer: Laws, rules or acts that violate the Constitution are *unconstitutional*.

Question: What does it mean if a law, rule or an act of a public official is unconstitutional?

Answer: Since the Constitution is the highest law of the land, anything *unconstitutional* is invalid—illegal and unenforceable.

The Bill of Rights

Question: What is the Bill of Rights?

Answer: Over the years additions and corrections to the Constitution have been made. These changes are known as *amendments*. The first ten amendments are known as the *Bill of Rights*. They define the rights of every individual and limit the power of the government over the people.

Throughout this book, there are references to the amendments. Those amendments are printed in the Appendix. They should be read and discussed whenever they are referred to in the text.

Case of the School Girl Scuffle

Assault and Battery

Case of the School Girl Scuffle

Carol Cruncher and Molly Meek had never been what you would call friends. In fact, you might call them enemies since Cruncher's old boyfriend, Howie Hunk, was now dating Molly.

One day after school, Carol Cruncher walked up to the corner where Molly Meek was talking to some friends. Cruncher was steaming.

"I should break your arm for stealing my boyfriend," she hissed.

> "Nobody can call me names and get away with it."

"What do you mean, steal?" Molly shot back. "Howie decided to stop seeing you because you are such a motor-mouth."

"Who's a motor-mouth? Nobody can call me names and get away with it. I'm going to slap some sense into you right now," said Cruncher, stepping forward menacingly, hand upraised.

It was a frightening move and Molly Meek was really scared. She stepped away without looking, stumbled backward and fell off the curb into the street. She hurt her arm in the fall and broke her brand-new watch.

"Look at what you've done," moaned Molly in tears. "You deliberately made me fall. Now you're in trouble. You're responsible for my arm and my watch!"

"Oh no I'm not," Cruncher responded with a snicker. "I never even touched you. Everybody could see that. And even if I did—you really had it coming for calling me a big mouth."

What's Your Opinion?

What's Your Opinion?

1. Did Carol Cruncher violate the law by threatening to strike Molly?

The Law Says:

Yes. Molly's threat was an assault. An assault is defined as an "imminent *threat* of physical harm when the victim reasonably believes that the assailant (attacker) is about to carry out the threat." Although the terms *assault and battery* are often used interchangeably, technically the assault is the threat or attempt. The battery is the actual physical contact.

What's Your Opinion?

2. Is any harmful physical contact with another person, without permission, a battery if it is done intentionally?

The Law Says:

Yes. Any hurtful or harmful touching without permssion is a battery, if done intentionally or very recklessly.

What's Your Opinion?

3. Are assault and battery violations of the criminal and/or civil law?

The Law Says:

Both. Minor assault and battery is a criminal misdemeanor. Serious assault and battery (with a weapon or one that causes serious injury) is a felony. One can also bring a civil lawsuit against an attacker to collect damages caused by the attack.

What's Your Opinion?

4. Can a verbal insult ever justify hitting someone?

The Law Says:

No. The law does not consider that any insult can justify a physical assault.

What's Your Opinion?

5. Is Carol Cruncher responsible legally for Molly's injured arm and broken watch?

The Law Says:

Yes. Even though Carol Cruncher didn't touch Molly Meek, Carol's threat was an assault which caused the injury.

What If?

1. **What If** a shouting match between the two girls resulted in Carol Cruncher's spitting in Molly's face? Would that be assault and battery? Explain.

   Answer: Yes. This is a case of assault and battery. Even though spitting is not a strong physical contact, it is still considered a battery. In defining a battery, the law does not indicate the degree of force that must be used, nor does it indicate what the striking must be done with. (See also answer 4.)

2. **What If** the assault and battery were committed with a baseball or a rock? Does this make a difference?

   Answer: Yes. Because these objects can create more serious injuries. Such an attack could be considered "assault with a deadly weapon," which is a felony—a more serious crime carrying greater penalties.

3. **What If** the two girls were arguing in the school yard and Carol Cruncher pulled a toy gun out of her pocket that looked like the real thing, and said, "I'm going to blow your head off!" Molly, terrified, fainted on the sidewalk. Is this an assault?

   Answer: Yes. Even though the weapon was a toy, if Molly reasonably believed it was real, this would be an assault. In some states it could even be considered an assault with a deadly weapon though that is not as likely.

4. **What If** Carol calls Molly a nerd and Molly, enraged, takes a swing at Carol but misses entirely? Was Molly guilty of assault?

   Answer: Yes. Though a minor assault which causes no damage would probably not be prosecuted by the police, such behavior by both parties could merit disciplinary action by a teacher or principal.

5. **What If** two people are arguing and one person gets so upset that he swings his fist and knocks off the other person's eyeglasses? Is this an assault and battery even if the striking party never physically touched the face of the person wearing the glasses?

   Answer: Definitely yes. This is an assault and batttery. Eyeglasses, clothing, jewelry and any other objects worn by a person are considered to be part of the body as far as the law of assault and battery is concerned.

6. **What If** Carol Cruncher backs Molly into a corner and there is no way out? Carol takes a swing at Molly. To ward off the attack, Molly lashes out and swings back hard, knocking Cruncher to the ground. Is Molly guilty of assault and battery?

   Answer: No, Molly is not guilty. The law recognizes that self-defense is appropriate to protect oneself from attack. Self-defense is the only justification that the law recognizes as a defense to assault and battery. But it is important to remember that one may not use more force in self-defense than absolutely necessary to repel the attack. And once the threat is gone the justification of self-defense is no longer available.

Activities

1. Are there other ways to settle the problems between Carol Cruncher and Molly Meek that could be tried instead of filing a lawsuit or a criminal complaint? What do you think could be done? Role-play a meeting between the girls, a counselor, parents or principal. The arrangement and the people involved are your choice. There may be one or more meetings to obtain a solution.

2. If you were given the task of establishing a Crisis Center to help students vent their anger and work things out constructively, how would it be organized? How could peer advisers be used along with adults? Write a paragraph or a page describing such a center. What could the people in such a center do to resolve conflict and avoid violence?

3. **You Be the Judge:** Role-play *The People vs. Robert B. Blaster*

   Police Report
   Date: October 20, 1987
   Location: Anytown, U.S.A.
   Officer: John Justice

   Facts: Bobby Blaster, age 13, was standing on the sidewalk in front of his house. It was a warm day. The front door to the house was wide open. Bobby had just come from a baseball game, and he was holding his favorite bat, "Old Faithful."

   Across the street, Norman Nasty (who has had several prior incidents with the police and is known as a bully) was yelling threats at Bobby such as, "You're a wimp, Blaster. I'm gonna come over there and clobber you."

   Nasty proceeded to shake his fist and walk slowly across the street toward Blaster, shouting insults all the while.

   Although he could have easily retreated into his house and slammed the door, Bobby chose to stand his ground. When Mr. Nasty got within range, Mr. Blaster bopped Nasty on the head with his bat once. It was a relatively light hit, but Nasty was knocked silly for several minutes before getting off the ground and running home.

   Complaining Witness: Norman Nasty

   Prosecutor's Recommendation
   Prosecutor: Lilly Lawful
   Date: October 21, 1987

   After reading Officer Justice's report, we have decided to charge Bobby Blaster with simple assault and battery (a misdemeanor). The reasons for charging Mr. Blaster are these:
   - Mr. Blaster struck Mr. Nasty with a baseball bat.
   - Mr. Blaster's use of the bat was greater force than what he was threatened with. Nor is it clear that Mr. Nasty was serious.

- Mr. Nasty never actually threw a punch (though he may have done so if he hadn't been struck by the bat first).
- Mr. Blaster could easily have retreated into his house. The law states that in such circumstances, one has a "duty to retreat." This means that if one is threatened with attack and it is possible to retreat to a place of safety before the attack, *one must do so*, before using deadly force (such as a bat).

The Prosecutor's office has decided to charge Mr. Blaster with simple misdemeanor assault rather than charge him with assault with a deadly weapon for these reasons:

a. Even though a bat might be considered a deadly weapon, in this case, Mr. Blaster tapped Mr. Nasty lightly, and just once.

b. We also took into consideration that Mr. Nasty started the trouble.

c. Mr. Blaster has no prior record.

You Be the Judge: Write a legal decision in the case of *The People of the City of Anytown vs. Robert B. Blaster.*

In your decision, discuss the facts of the case, the law of assault and battery, and the question of whether Bobby acted in self-defense. Think about the "duty to retreat" and why it is a part of the law.

Finally, you must decide whether Bobby is guilty (beyond a reasonable doubt) of assault and battery or not guilty because he acted in justifiable self-defense.*

If you find Bobby guilty, you must decide what sentence (punishment) to impose.

*Note: If Bobby claims he acted in self-defense, the prosecutor must prove, beyond a reasonable doubt, that Bobby did not act in self-defense, in order for Bobby to be guilty.

4. **Discussion:** After understanding the definition of the "duty to retreat," explain why you think the law has evolved this way. Write a statement of agreement or disagreement with the doctrine. Support your point of view.

(**Answer:** The law created the duty to retreat in order to minimize violence whenever possible. In this case, Bobby is probably guilty [although some judges or juries might find him not guilty]. Although this is a close case, the authors believe Mr. Blaster guilty for three reasons: (a) He could have easily retreated into his house (b) Blaster used more force to repel the attack than what he was threatened with, and (c) it isn't clear that Norman Nasty was actually about to assault Bobby Blaster.)

Alternate Activity: Hold a mock jury trial in the case of *The People vs. Bobby Blaster* using the format described in "Case of the Reluctant Donation." Only the witness cards and charge need to be changed.

Case of the Bicycle Blunder

Case of the Bicycle Blunder

It was a busy Saturday afternoon in the business district of Anytown. Claude Klutz pulled up to the supermarket with his scarf flying. In a hurry as usual, he left his new Moto-Cross bike lying down on the sidewalk, right smack in front of the automatic doors. Bustling out of the store carrying three big bags, came Greta Golightly, whose arms were loaded. She could not see over her groceries and certainly couldn't see the bike lying in her path. Nor did

> **She put her foot through the spokes of Klutz's front wheel.**

she expect to encounter any obstruction lying on the sidewalk that would interfere with foot traffic in and out of the store. Before she realized what had happened, she had put her foot through the spokes of Claude's front wheel. Groceries went flying everywhere and so did Ms. Golightly. Claude Klutz heard the commotion on his way out and saw a woman sprawled on the ground on top of his wrecked bike!

"You've ruined my wheel! Why did you have to do that?" he yelled.

"I just about killed myself on your bike and that's all you have to say?" she shouted back, stumbling to her feet.

"You owe me for a new wheel," Claude insisted.

"I've got news for you, buddy! You owe me for all these ruined groceries, and you might owe me for a broken leg," griped Greta.

What's Your Opinion?

What's Your Opinion?

1. Who is wrong in this case? Explain.

The Law Says:

Claude Klutz is wrong. His wrongful act is legally known as a *tort* (*tort* means "wrong" in French). Claude has committed a tort because (a) he was negligent and (b) his negligence caused harm to Greta. Negligence means Claude neglected (breached) his duty to be reasonably careful. Another word for negligence is *carelessness*. Negligence is the legal word for carelessness. Claude's negligence makes him liable for Greta's damages.

What's Your Opinion?

2. What duty did Claude have to Greta Golightly in this case?

The Law Says:

Claude had a duty to Ms. Golightly and all other people who could reasonably be expected to be shopping. His duty was to park his bike carefully so that it was out of the way.

What's Your Opinion?

3. Must Greta Golightly pay for the damage she did to Claude's bike?

The Law Says:

No. Greta is not liable (responsible) in this case because she was not negligent. She had no responsibility to avoid a bike that should not have been there in the first place. Though she did damage Claude's bike, since she is not negligent, she did not commit a tort and need not pay for the damage.

What's Your Opinion?

4. Can Claude Klutz be held responsible for Greta Golightly's injuries even if he is a minor?

The Law Says:

Yes. Minors can be held responsible for their torts if the court finds that they were old enough to know better (to know they should have been more careful under the circumstances, given their age and experience).

What's Your Opinion?

5. If Claude has no money, how can Greta collect from him for her damages?

The Law Says:

In some states Claude's parents might be held responsible for Claude's negligent behavior. (See "Case of the Beer Bust.") Also, if Greta sues Claude and wins, the *judgment* (decision in her favor) is good for up to ten years. That means Greta can collect money on her judgment when Claude gets a job or earns any income during the ten years following the judgment.

What's Your Opinion?

6. Claude has committed a tort. A tort is a civil wrong. Is Claude Klutz also guilty of a crime?

The Laws Says:

No. In this case, Claude's act is not a crime because it was not done intentionally or recklessly. It was an accident caused by carelessness.

What's Your Opinion?

7. Can a wrongful act be both a tort and a crime? Under what circumstances?

The Law Says:

Yes. Some wrongful acts can be both a civil tort and a crime if they are done intentionally or very recklessly. Intentional torts are more serious than negligent torts. Such acts can be prosecuted criminally and also pursued in a civil lawsuit.

What's Your Opinion?

8. Assault and battery, malicious destruction of property, and sometimes trespassing are intentional torts that are also crimes. Why do you think intentional torts are considered more serious than negligent torts?

The Law Says:

When someone injures a person or their property by accident, it is not considered as mean or dangerous an act as when someone intentionally tries to do harm, or when their recklessness causes harm.

What If?

1. **What If** Claude is riding his bike carefully on the street and Greta Golightly steps off the curb into his path without looking? Claude hits her, damaging his bike and Greta's groceries. Who is negligent then? Why?

   Answer: In that case, Greta is negligent. She neglected her duty to look both ways before walking into the street. Claude was not negligent if he was operating his bike safely since he had the "right of way" and would not expect Greta to walk off the curb without looking. Greta has committed the tort in this case.

2. **What If** Claude is riding his bike down the street on a clear, sunny day? Suddenly, a surprise gust of wind blows his bike off course and he strikes Greta who was crossing the street several feet away. Would either party be responsible to pay for the other's damages? Why?

   Answer: In this case neither party is responsible. Since the gust of wind was an unforeseeable surprise, there is no negligence by either party and therefore no tort and no liability by either.

Activities

1. We are all responsible for our own behavior. We all have a duty to be reasonably careful to avoid injuring other people or their property. List the duties a reasonable person would have while doing the following:

   - Riding a bicycle or skateboard.
   - Playing on the playground.
   - Driving an automobile.
   - Cooking food in a restaurant.
   - Delivering papers in a neighborhood.
   - Shooting a BB rifle.
   - Playing football, baseball, hockey, soccer, etc.
   - Building a tree house.
   - Inviting people into your home.
   - Going swimming.
   - Repairing a friend's bicycle.

2. A local storekeeper, Mr. Mercantile, is sick and tired of the kids leaving their bikes outside the entrance when coming in after school. Their bikes block the way so other customers can't get in. Angrily, the storekeeper posts a sign on the door that reads, "Absolutely No Students Allowed Until After 5:00 p.m." Some of the students just grumble but others want to do something constructive about the problem. Role-play a scene with the students making a plan. How can they negotiate with Mr. Mercantile so that they may be permitted to shop in the store after school, as before? Assign roles, as well, to those who do not believe there is a solution.

Case of the Heavy Chevy

Case of the Heavy Chevy

Fabulous Frankie Farbush had just turned sixteen and the very first thing he did on his birthday was apply for a driver's license. On his way back home, Frankie spotted a really sweet old Chevy parked in the driveway of the Hardnose house. It had a big *For Sale* sign in the windshield. Frankie fell madly in love with it. He knocked on the door of the house and Harriet Hardnose answered. She explained that she wanted $450 for the car and it was a real

> "A deal is a deal. I'm keeping the deposit."

bargain. Frankie almost passed out with excitement and shouted, "It's a deal." At that moment he was positive he could manage the finances. Hardnose said she wanted a deposit to hold the car. She wrote a contract which read:

> Sold by Harriet Hardnose, to Frankie Farbush, for $450 for her red Chevrolet. A nonrefundable deposit of $50 will hold the car for seven days at which time Farbush will pay the $400 balance and own the car.

They both signed the agreement. Frankie made his way back home, dizzy with the thrill of it. Wait till his friends saw him in that vintage car! He would work and slave to pay for the car. Maybe his dad would help him. As he approached his house, a cloud of doubt began to descend. When Frankie told his parents what he had done, his father was furious. They rushed back to the Hardnose place where his dad demanded the $50 deposit be returned.

"A deal is a deal," Hardnose reminded him. "Look at what it says in the contract—*nonrefundable*, and Frankie here signed it. I'm sorry, but I'm keeping the deposit for my trouble. Besides, right after Frankie left, another customer turned up who wanted to pay cash. I could've sold it on the spot. But I turned down the chance on account of the deposit!"

What's Your Opinion?

What's Your Opinion?
1. What is a contract?

The Law Says:
A contract is a legally binding agreement between two or more people (or businesses), exchanging one thing of value for another. This exchange is known in Latin as *quid pro quo*, which translates as "something for something."

What's Your Opinion?
2. Did Harriet Hardnose and Frankie Farbush enter into a contract?

The Law Says:
Yes. Frankie agreed to pay $450 in exchange for Harriet selling him the car.

What's Your Opinion?
3. Was the contract valid and enforceable? Explain.

The Law Says:
No. Since Frankie was under 18, he was not yet legally an adult. As a minor, he could not enter into an enforceable contract.

What's Your Opinion?
4. Must Harriet return Frankie's deposit?

The Law Says:
Yes. Contracts with minors are *voidable* by the minor or his parents, and since Frankie's father made Frankie void the contract, Ms. Hardnose has no legal right to keep the money. (*Void* means to have no legal effect; as if the contract never existed.)

What's Your Opinion?
5. What is it called when one party breaks a valid contract or does not live up to his end of a bargain?

The Law Says:
Failure to perform, in whole or in part, is called a "breach of contract."

What's Your Opinion?
6. Can a contract be oral?

The Law Says:
Yes. Contracts for small amounts of money, which can be carried out in less than a year, can be valid even if they are not in writing. Some contracts, however, such as land sales contracts, are not valid unless they are in writing.

What's Your Opinion?

7. What kinds of problems arise with oral contracts?

The Law Says:

Oral contracts are hard to enforce because it is hard to determine exactly what the terms are. It is often hard to prove that the contract even existed if one of the parties contests it. It is always a good idea to put any agreement into writing to avoid confusion and misunderstanding.

What's Your Opinion?

8. Did Frankie Farbush breach a contract with Ms. Hardnose?

The Law Says:

No. Only a valid contract can be breached. Frankie's contract was voided, not breached.

What If?

1. **What If** Ms. Hardnose had let Frankie take the car before he paid for it? Since he was a minor, would he have to pay for the car on the unenforceable (void) contract?

   Answer: He would either have to return the car or pay for it. Even though the contract was not valid, once Frankie had the car in his possession the law would not let him be "unjustly enriched," which means it is unlawful to profit from an improper deal.

2. **What If** Frankie Farbush, who is sixteen, had signed a contract with Ms. Hardnose to buy a winter coat on a freezing cold day? Would that contract be enforceable by either party?

   Answer: Yes. Certain contracts made by minors are enforceable for important reasons of public policy. Minors can legally contract for the necessities of life—food, clothing and shelter. Certain other contracts by minors are also valid (auto insurance and enlisting in the armed forces).

3. **What If** your dad needs 500 apples to make caramel apples for your school's Halloween party? He signs a contract with Sam's Fruit Store to buy the apples for $100. Sam agrees to deliver the apples before the party. The day before the party Sam tells your dad that his truck broke down and he can't deliver the apples in time, but he will drop off the apples the day after Halloween. Your dad knows that will be too late. Dad buys the apples elsewhere for $150. Who is responsible for the extra $50 your dad pays?

   Answer: Sam, the store owner, is responsible to pay your dad the $50. This is the *difference* between the contract price and the price your dad finally had to pay. The $50 is known as "difference damages." Even though Sam's failure to deliver the apples on time was not his fault, he will be held to his contractual promise to perform and must pay the consequences if he breaches his promise.

Activities

1. Arrange to work with a partner to write a contract. A contract has to be "bargained for." This agreement may be for a service or may involve the sale of an object. Specify who the contracting parties are. What is the time for the performance of the contract? When writing a good contract, it is important to anticipate problems in advance and try to avoid them.

2. "Time is of the essence" is a term that is used when referring to a contract. What do you think it means? Why is it important that people perform their end of a bargain when they say they will? Give examples.

3. It is not necessary for money to change hands in a contract. The contracting parties might exchange services. What is most important is that there be an exchange of something of value. In fact—sometimes an agreement not to do something can be the basis of a contract. This means that the nonaction of one of the parties must be of value to the other party. For example, sometimes farmers are paid by the government not to plant crops. The value is that crop prices will remain stable, if there is not a surplus, and that the land will not be overused. Given this information, what agreements could be reached by people not to do something? A classic contract between you and your parents not to do something could be this: If you stop biting your nails, your dad will buy you a watch. Think of other nonaction contracts to negotiate between you and members of your family or friends.

4. **Role Play:** Sports figures, singers, dancers, actors, writers and people in all walks of life enter into contracts. Choose a favorite celebrity and negotiate, with a tough adversary, for a really good contract. Role-play as if you were the agent and you want your client to gain the most advantage possible. Who is the person you are negotiating with?

5. **Role Play:** You are the manager of the Anytown Music Hall. On the date of a scheduled appearance, the musical group you contracted with does not show up. The hall has been sold out of tickets. Get on the telephone and inform the group's agent that you are going to sue for *damages*. What would you say? What do you think the agent and the musical group are responsible for (lost ticket sales, rent, stagehands' wages, etc.)? Have the band's agent argue that the band is not responsible. Discuss what damages caused by the band's breach of contract are too remote (or unreasonable) to be charged to the band.

Case of the Forgotten Fudge

Case of the Forgotten Fudge

After school, Nina Nibbler decides to go to Hagelstein's Department Store to pick up some school supplies. While she is there she buys a loose-leaf notebook, some index cards and a yellow marker. As she passes the candy counter, the smell of freshly popped corn reminds her that she is starting to feel hunger pangs. Quickly looking over the displayed goodies, she sees a luscious wrapped block of Mackinac chocolate fudge and decides that it

> **"I had every intention of paying for the fudge!"**

looks so delicious she simply can't resist it. As usual, she has selected more items than she anticipated and has not taken a basket. Because her hands are full of odds and ends, she does a balancing act and slips the fudge into her coat pocket, fully intending to pay for it. Before she can even get to the checkout counter, she feels the weight of a big hand on her shoulder.

"I saw that, young lady," says a large man, looking directly into her face. "Come with me. You're under arrest for shoplifting."

Nina feels her heart constrict and start to beat like a trip hammer. "Oh no," she protests, "I had every intention of paying for the fudge!"

What's Your Opinion?

What's Your Opinion?

1. Can the store detective arrest Nina Nibbler?

The Law Says:

Yes. A store owner or the agent of the owner can make a citizen's arrest for crimes committed in their presence. If the arrest is not reasonable or is extremely improper, the person arrested has the right to file a lawsuit later. Reasonableness is the key. If the attempted arrest is unreasonable, the store may be liable in court for committing a "false arrest."

What's Your Opinion?

2. Would this be a legitimate arrest even though Nina did not intend to steal the fudge and she had not left the store?

The Law Says:

In most states, yes. The crime of larceny or attempted larceny is determined by several factors. One necessary element of the crime is the *intent to permanently deprive the rightful owner of his possession.* In many states it is not absolutely necessary to leave the premises to be found guilty. However, it will be more difficult for the store to prove its case in court since Nina did not actually try to leave the store without paying.

What's Your Opinion?

3. Is Nina guilty of larceny?

The Law Says:

No. Larceny requires the intent to steal (to deprive the owner of an object without paying for it). Nina had no such intent. She is not guilty.

What's Your Opinion?

4. What should you do if you believe you are being arrested or searched unlawfully by a police officer?

The Law Says:

Clearly state your objections to the actions and then peacefully submit. It is never wise to try to physically resist an arrest performed by a police officer, even if it is an unlawful arrest. If it is unlawful, the products of the search will be excluded as evidence and you may have a case for filing a suit for false arrest. The only time one should resist an "arrest" is if you feel that someone is using the word *arrest,* as an excuse to kidnap or molest you.

What's Your Opinion?

5. After the police have taken her into custody and made a report, can they continue to keep Nina at the police station?

The Law Says:

If she is a minor and has committed a nonviolent crime, in most states the police must contact her parents as soon as possible and release her to the custody of her parents until a hearing or trial in juvenile court. If Nina is an adult, the police must release her on "bail." (See the Eighth Amendment to the U.S. Constitution.)

What's Your Opinion?

6. The police arrive at the store. The store detective tells his side of the story to the police officer. The officer tells Nina that she is under arrest for larceny for stealing a fifty-cent piece of fudge and tells her to hand it over. She refuses. Can the police officer arrest and search her without a warrant?

The Law Says:

This is a trickier question than it appears on the surface because in some states shoplifting is a misdemeanor and in some states it is a felony.

If the crime is a misdemeanor, unless it is committed in the presence of the officer, he cannot lawfully arrest and search an adult without a warrant from a judge. If Nina is a juvenile, an officer may "detain" her in "protective custody" but not search her without a warrant. (In truth, this "detention" is effectively an arrest.)

If the crime is a felony, a police officer can arrest and search a suspect, even if the crime was not committed in the presence of the officer, if the officer has *probable cause* to believe (a) that a felony was committed and (b) that the suspect committed it. (See the Fourth Amendment of the U.S. Constitution.)

These standards are designed to limit the power of the police.

What If?

1. **What If** Nina Nibbler had totally *forgotten* the fudge and walked out of the store without paying for it, though she had paid for the other merchandise? What would happen if she were arrested? Would she be guilty of larceny (shoplifting)?

   Answer: No. In this situation, for Nina's act to be a crime she must have specifically *intended* to steal the fudge. If Nina is prosecuted and pleads innocent, a judge would have to decide whether or not she had the *intent* and whether all other elements of the crime of larceny were also present beyond a reasonable doubt.

2. **What If** Nina had paid for all her purchases, including the fudge, but then was seen putting the fudge into her pocket and was stopped by a suspicious store detective? What could she do?

   Answer: She could produce her sales receipt to prove that she had paid for the fudge. A receipt is a legal document! Always put your purchase in a bag and always wait for your sales receipt, which is your proof of purchase, no matter how small the item may be.

3. **What If** you go to the supermarket after school and are shopping from a list of groceries your dad gave you? As you wend your way through the aisles, you realize that you are starving and start snacking. You open some packages of sweet and salty treats in your cart to hold off the hunger. The manager comes up to you and asks you to come to the office for shoplifting. You protest that you only ate a few small, insignificant items, and they were from packages you were going to buy. You insist that they are being ridiculous. Can they really charge you with larceny?

Answer: They can try, though it will not be a strong case. The practical lesson here is that you should always avoid even the appearance of taking something that doesn't yet belong to you. Do not eat food or put things in your pocket before you pay for them, even though you intend to purchase them. Appearances do count! Remember, you can sometimes lose a case even though you are innocent. Even if you are found innocent by a judge after a trial, it is not worth going through all the hassle just because you were absentminded.

Activities

1. The cost to society of petty larceny is much higher than the mere price of the stolen objects. Pretend you are an investigative reporter. Explain in an article how the cost of shoplifting is passed on to the consumer in higher prices. (The owner of a store must make up the losses from the stolen merchandise, by having to pay wages to security people, installing TV monitors, and other preventative systems.) Consider also the high costs of administering the criminal justice system (police, courts, judges and jails). Your article may be headed, "Crime Has Many Consequences."

2. Someone steals your homework. It is written on a piece of paper worth only 1/3 cent. Would you consider it a fair deal if the punishment to the thief was to pay a fine of 1/3 cent? Write your reaction to this. The punishment for larceny may be to pay a fine far greater than the value of the stolen object. Why? (**Answer:** Deterrence and costs noted in number one above.)

3. Lester Loophole sees a car at the curb with a key in the ignition. He has taken a course entitled, "Everyday Law for Young Citizens." He remembers that one of the elements of larceny is that the person committing the larceny must intend to *permanently* deprive the owner of the use and possession of the item taken. (Unfortunately, Lester Loophole skipped several of the classes!) He decides to take the car for a quick ride. He intends to return the car when he is done and assumes that this is not larceny. Is Lester correct in assuming that this is not larceny? (**Answer:** Yes, he is correct.) Is it another crime? Explain. (**Answer:** It is a crime called "joy riding.") This occurrence is common and in the past seemed to fall between the cracks of the law. Therefore the lawmakers decided to close this loophole and create a law to cover these situations. What is meant by the figure of speech *loophole?*

4. Consider your own personal safety. You are in a store. A person approaches you and claims to be a store detective who suspects you of shoplifting. What should you do or say to protect yourself?

   Role-play a scene using the above facts.

   Suggestions: • Consider the outside possibility that the person trying to arrest you may not be who he claims to be and may have other motives for detaining you.

   • Always ask for identification.

   • Never leave the store with anyone but a real police officer.

   • Make sure that the management or police contact your parents as soon as possible—even though it may be embarrassing.

5. The police arrive at the store. Before doing anything else, the police officer asks you for your name or identification. Must you respond? Explain the practical and legal reasons why you must identify yourself even if you are innocent. (**Answer:** If you are being accused of a minor crime, if you identify yourself the police officer will often just release you or release you to your parents even if you may be later charged with the crime. If the officer does not know who you are or where you live, he may have no choice but to take you into custody just to find out who you are.) However, you need not respond to any other questions.

6. **After You Are Arrested:** You give your name to the police and they call your parents. If your parents give their permission for you to be questioned, the police must still tell you one more thing before asking you any more questions. Do you know what they must tell you? (**Answer:** The police must tell you what your rights are. These are often called "Miranda rights," because the U.S. Supreme Court defined these rights in a case called *Miranda vs. Arizona* 384 U.S. 436 [1966].) Do you know what the Miranda rights are? You may have seen police warn suspects on television this way. Can you repeat them?

   - You have the right to remain silent.
   - You have the right to an attorney.
   - If you cannot afford an attorney one will be appointed for you at public expense.
   - If you decide to make a statement, anything you say may be used against you in a court of law.

7. Which amendments to the Constitution, in the Bill of Rights, guarantee the rights listed in the Miranda warnings? (**Answer:** Part of the Fifth and Sixth Amendments.)

Case of the Beer Bust

Case of the Beer Bust

Moe and Curly's parents were out of town. The boys decided that this was the perfect time to have a big party at their folks' cottage on the lake. The plan was informal and the invitations circulated by word of mouth. The news swept the school and on the appointed evening there were more guests than they had expected. As a matter of fact there were lots of faces that Moe and Curly didn't even recognize! Some good sports came with chips, soft drinks and assorted munchies. Moe and Curly made sure there was a big supply of beer. The noise began to escalate and before too long the party was out of control, with more than a few people getting seriously drunk. Close to midnight, a carload of unsteady kids left the house heading toward town. Unfortunately they didn't make it all the way. The car went out of control and struck and seriously injured a pedestrian walking on the sidewalk.

> **Before too long the party was out of control.**

The injured person, Henry Hapless, decided from his wheelchair, that he was going to sue to compensate for the enormous medical expenses as well as for his pain, suffering and loss of income.

What's Your Opinion?

What's Your Opinion?

1. Who is legally responsible for Henry's injuries?

The Law Says:

The driver of the car is responsible because (a) he caused Henry's injuries and (b) the driver was negligent. Negligence means that the driver neglected to do something he had a duty to do—which was to drive carefully. Less obviously Moe and Curly are also very likely to be held responsible since they supplied the beer that contributed to the driver's intoxication.

What's Your Opinion?

2. What can the pedestrian do if he decides to sue Moe and Curly and finds out that they are minors (under the age of 18) with no money of their own?

The Law Says:

The pedestrian can file a claim or lawsuit against Moe and Curly's parents. Many states and cities have passed laws explicitly holding parents liable for the irresponsible and unsupervised acts of their minor children. More and more courts are also holding people responsible for damages caused by guests who become drunk at parties in their homes.

What's Your Opinion?

3. Did Moe and Curly and their friends commit any crimes in this case? If so, what crimes were committed?

The Law Says:

Yes. Serving alcohol to minors is a crime. Minors who possess or consume alcohol are committing a crime in most states. Driving while under the influence of alcohol (drunk driving) is a crime. Injuring the pedestrian, Henry Hapless, is "criminal negligence," due to the extremely reckless behavior of the drunk driver.

What's Your Opinion?

4. How can injuring someone accidentally be a crime if crimes require criminal intent?

The Law Says:

If one acts in an extremely reckless or dangerous manner which injures other people, the law assumes that one knows that such behavior is likely to cause injury. Therefore, the law says that one who injures another due to recklessness had a "general intent" to cause the injury even though it was an "accident." The law considers reckless behavior more blameworthy than ordinary negligence.

What's Your Opinion?

5. Why are the manufacture, sale, and use of food, drugs, chemicals, alcoholic beverages, tobacco and firearms more tightly controlled by the government than sales of other substances?

The Law Says:

Because some substances and products are dangerous if not properly produced and used. The government makes laws to control their use and manufacture to insure the public health and welfare.

What If?

1. **What If** Moe and Curly did not supply the alcohol at the party, but did not stop others from drinking it? Would they and their parents still be responsible for the pedestrian's injury?

   Answer: It is still very likely that a judge or jury would find Moe and Curly and their parents responsible since Moe and Curly hosted the party and allowed alcohol to be consumed.

2. **What If** we lived in a country where there were no laws at all that regulated the production or manufacture or use of anything? What would be the result?

   Answer: Chaos would result with serious harm done to many people. There would be many more accidents caused by drunk driving or driving under the influence of drugs. Our environment would become more polluted if manufacturers were not held responsible for the noxious waste products they produced. Foods would be less pure if manufacturers were not held responsible for the inspection of food products and for the prevention of contamination of those food products. More people would die of lung cancer caused by air pollution and cigarettes. More people would be killed and injured by faulty products. There would be no safety outside your home or even in your home.

3. **What If** the pedestrian, Henry Hapless, or a passenger in the car had been killed in the accident? Would the driver be guilty of murder?

   Answer: Not exactly. The death would be considered a *homicide* (meaning any killing of a person by another person). *Murder* is a homicide committed intentionally. Murder is often divided into categories. The law considers the worst type of murder ("first degree murder") to require premeditation (planning). Second degree murder is intentional but not planned in advance. (Killing someone in the heat of an argument is second degree murder.)

   Homicides resulting from auto accidents are usually classified as *manslaughter* if recklessness is involved. Manslaughter, like drunk driving, is a crime resulting from extreme recklessness. Manslaughter is a crime of "general intent." Murder requires "specific intent."

   In this case, the driver would be guilty of manslaughter.

FINIS

Activities

1. Role-play a party at your home. You try to stop your good friend when you find out he has brought in beer and has started drinking it. All of a sudden your friend acts like he is Macho Man. What can you say to him, and how can you say it, to stop him? As he gets louder, you and your guests try to work out this problem.

2. Write a list of suggestions for parents, teachers, and others in the community that would help reduce drinking and other kinds of substance abuse. Is there a greater problem at school dances and athletic events? Explain your answer. Can you describe a preventative program in your school district or any other you have heard about? How can these programs be improved?

3. With a partner, write a law which you think would regulate alcohol. Include sections on supplying alcohol to minors. Read these laws aloud. Decide who wrote the fairest and most complete law. Could these laws be enforced?

4. Read about alcohol and its effects on the mind and body. Find at least one piece of information that you never knew before (alcohol is a drug, a twelve-ounce can of beer has the same amount of alcohol as a one-ounce glass of whiskey). Contribute to a fact-finding session in class. As a good research person, give the title of the book, magazine, pamphlet or newspaper used as your source. Include the copyright date, the page number, the publisher, and the city. Why is the copyright date important when one is dealing with information? (**Answer:** Current information is more reliable.) What is the minimum legal age in your state for the purchase of alcoholic beverages?

5. Research the national organization called SADD, Students Against Drunk Driving, which was founded in 1981. The organization is a network of students and parents who lobby for more effective legislation against drunk driving and urge strong penalties. They aim to increase public awareness and to take action. They conduct research, compile statistics and maintain a speaker's bureau. They have a publication: *SADD in Your School.* Write to SADD, P.O. Box 800, Marlboro, MA 07152, (301) 937-7936.

6. Define *controlled substance.* (**Answer:** A controlled substance is any material or product whose manufacture, sale and/or use is controlled or regulated by laws [insecticides, prescription drugs, illegal drugs, tobacco, guns, alcoholic beverages, fuels, chemicals].) Brainstorm a list of controlled substances on a chart or on the board.

If some substances are so dangerous, why are they allowed to be used at all? (**Answer:** Because they are also beneficial. They are also a source of profit and tax revenue. Some substances, such as heroin and the insecticide D.D.T. are so dangerous or provide so little benefit that the law makes them completely illegal.) What do you think are the dangers and benefits of controlled substances you've listed?

Construct a chart which illustrates controlled substances and their dangers and benefits.

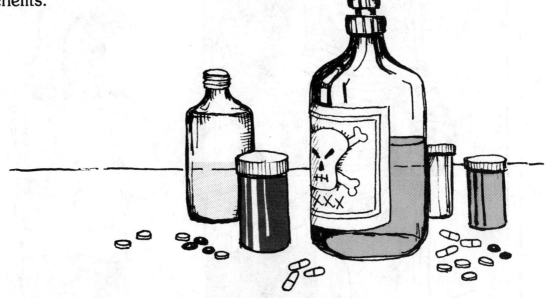

Additional Information for the Teacher

- Foods are inspected to insure the purity of what we eat.
- Prescription drugs are regulated to guarantee purity and to avoid misuse or abuse.
- Production and sale of chemicals are regulated to control waste produced when they are manufactured and to insure that chemicals are not improperly used.
- Fuels such as coal and gasoline are inspected for purity to minimize the toxic gasses that result from their combustion. Bad fuels can damage the machines that burn them. Gasoline is explosive if improperly used.
- Alcoholic beverages are regulated both to insure that they are properly produced and also to avoid use by minors and abuse by adults.
- Firearms are regulated so that extremely dangerous weapons such as machine guns do not get into the hands of criminals.
- Insecticides must be used only in approved ways in order to prevent harm to humans and animals. Insecticides are tested and regulated to minimize dangerous and unpredictable side effects on the environment.
- Hazardous building products such as asbestos, solvents and glue are regulated to reduce exposure of workers and consumers. A prime example of this is the stricter regulation and removal of asbestos (which can cause lung cancer) which was used widely in schools and offices as insulation.

Case of the Reluctant Donation

Larceny from a Person/Robbery

Case of the Reluctant Donation

Betsy Bystander was minding her own business in the halls of Anytown High when she saw the approach of Stella Strongarm, one of the more threatening students in the school. Stella was always trouble. Betsy tried her best to become part of the wall and blend in with the background, but it didn't work. She had once read something about how not to look like a victim, but she couldn't remember the advice—besides, Stella was coming toward her like a steamroller.

> **"... hand one over, if you know what's good for you!"**

"Hey, Baby Face, I need a quarter and I need it right now, so just hand one over if you know what's good for you!"

Betsy backed away from the sneering Stella Strongarm. "If I give you a quarter, I won't have enough for lunch!" she pleaded.

"That's not my problem now is it, Chubkins? Just hand it over, or else . . . ."

Betsy, feeling as if she had no choice, dug down into her jacket pocket, withdrew the quarter, and gave it to the looming Stella Strongarm, who walked away laughing.

What's Your Opinion?

What's Your Opinion?

1. *Larceny* means taking away someone else's property unlawfully with the intention of permanently depriving the owner of its use. *Robbery* means taking property from a person by force or fear. Was Stella's behavior criminal? If so, what crime was committed?

The Law Says:

Yes. Her behavior was criminal because she forced Betsy Bystander to give her money. Although there was no overt threat of force, it was implied by her manner ("if you know what's good for you" and "just hand it over, or else"). Stella was guilty of "unarmed robbery"—also known as "larceny from a person."

What's Your Opinion?

2. Remember, a *felony* is a criminal act. It is a more serious crime than a misdemeanor. It is punishable by imprisonment for longer than a year. A *misdemeanor* is a criminal act. It is a crime less serious than a felony and may be punishable by imprisonment for less than a year. Why is "petty larceny" a misdemeanor while larceny from a person is a felony, even if the amount of money taken is small?

The Law Says:

Robbery involves taking money or valuables directly from a person with violence or threats of violence. The law considers crimes of violence against people more serious than crimes against property.

What If?

1. **What If** Stella Strongarm had said, "Lend me a quarter," instead of "Give me a quarter"? Would that still be a crime?

   Answer: This is a closer question, which would depend upon whether Stella had intended to return the money or whether her behavior was merely a dishonest strategy.

2. **What If** Stella Strongarm sees that her neighbor is out mowing the lawn. Stella quickly goes around to the rear of her neighbor's house, quietly opens the back screen door and slips into the empty kitchen. In a flash, she grabs a $5 bill off the kitchen table and sneaks out quickly! Is this crime a felony or a misdemeanor? Why?

   Answer: In most states this crime would be considered the felony of "breaking and entering." The law considers it to be a more serious crime when one unlawfully enters a building to commit a larceny, even though a small amount of money may be involved. Breaking and entering does not literally mean the felon must break anything. Slipping in through a window or unlocked door can still be considered breaking and entering.

Activity
The Trial of Stella Strongarm

Hold a mock trial in the case of *The People of the City of Anytown vs. Stella Strongarm*. Appoint a prosecuting attorney to represent the City and Betsy Bystander, a defense attorney to represent Stella Strongarm, a judge (perhaps the teacher), a bailiff, and a court clerk. One student will be Stella (the defendant) and one student will be Betsy Bystander (the complaining witness). There may also be several other witnesses—some friendly to Stella, some friendly to Betsy. Stella is over 18 and is therefore being tried as an adult, in front of a jury. The two attorneys will pick a jury (of 6 or 12) from members of the class. All prospective jurors will be asked questions to make sure they are not biased. This process is called *voir dire* pronounced "vwor deer," which means in French "to speak the truth." Any juror who appears to be biased will be eliminated at the discretion of the judge, at the request of either attorney. To add interest, hand out Bias Cards (below) to prospective jurors as role-play clues. You may allow the prospective jurors to hide their biases, but not lie, if asked questions by either attorney that brings their biases to light. Attorneys cannot merely ask: "Do you have any biases," but must ask specific questions such as: "Does any juror know the Defendant, the Plaintiff, or their families?" The judge may also "voir dire" jurors.

Juror Bias Cards
(Assign only one bias per potential juror.)

You may be biased in favor of the prosecution and the complaining witness, Betsy Bystander, because:
- You believe that if Stella is in court, she must be guilty.
- You don't like Stella's looks.
- You were once mugged on the street.
- Your mother had her purse snatched once.
- You are a police officer.
- You know Betsy's family.
- You read a story in the newspaper about this case that sounded like Stella was guilty.

You may be biased in favor of the defendant, Stella Strongarm, because:
- You were once convicted of shoplifting unfairly.
- You work for Stella's father.
- You were once sued by Betsy Bystander's family.
- You are a criminal defense lawyer.
- You are a friend of the defense lawyer.
- You believe that no one should go to jail for property crimes.
- You believe that Betsy looks like a liar.

Teacher: Most potential jurors should receive a card that says: "You are not biased." Remind the jurors that, if chosen, they must try to set aside their biases. If a juror is eliminated for bias, a new juror is chosen from the pool until all sides agree that the jury is acceptable.

The Role of the Bailiff: The bailiff "swears in" the witnesses by saying, "Please raise your right hand. Do you solemnly swear to tell the truth, the whole truth, and nothing but the truth, so help you God?"

When the judge or jury enters or leaves, the bailiff asks the observers in the courtroom to "Please rise." When the jury is seated, the bailiff says to the entire courtroom, "Please be seated." At the beginning of the session, when the judge enters, the bailiff loudly says, "All rise. District Court for the City of Anytown, the Honorable Judge (teacher's name) presiding, is now in session. Please be seated."

The Court Recorder: The court recorder makes an exact transcript of every word spoken during the proceedings on a stenotype machine. In this case, an approximation of the proceedings will be fine.

The Judge: The judge reads the charges to the Defendant, Stella Strongarm. "You are charged with the crime of larceny from a person, also known as unarmed robbery. If convicted, you will face a sentence of up to three years in jail and a fine up to $1,000. How do you plead?"

The defendant pleads "not guilty." (Had she pled "guilty," there would be no trial.) After a jury is chosen, the prosecutor and defense attorney each make opening statements to support their cases. Witnesses testify after being sworn in by the bailiff. The prosecutor starts first because the prosecution has the burden of proving the guilt of the defendant. A defendant is innocent until proven guilty.

The prosecutor calls Betsy Bystander and her witnesses individually to the stand for "direct examination." The defense attorney then "cross-examines" the witnesses.

The defense attorney then calls Stella Strongarm and her witnesses to the stand for "direct exam" followed by the prosecutor's "cross-exam."* Any evidence is introduced and marked as exhibits (such as the money Stella Strongarm took). Testimony can be given from the police officer who investigated the case.

After the prosecution and the defense "rest" their cases, they are allowed to make closing arguments to the jury. This is the last chance for each attorney to try to convince the jury to decide in favor of his/her client.

The Judge then instructs the jury. "Stella Strongarm is innocent until proven guilty. If you find *beyond a reasonable doubt* that Stella Strongarm is guilty of the crime of larceny from a person, you must find her guilty. If you have *any reasonable doubt* about her intent to permanently deprive the plaintiff, Betsy Bystander, of her money, you must find the defendant, Stella Strongarm, not guilty. Remember, Stella is charged with larceny from a person, also known as robbery. To be guilty, it must be proven beyond a reasonable doubt that Stella did force Betsy Bystander to give Stella money against Betsy's will. Now you, the jury, will deliberate in private. Pick a foreperson who will chair your discussion and who will tell the court when you have reached a decision and what that decision is. You may now deliberate." (In some states the jury verdict in a criminal trial must be unanimous. In other states it is only required that eleven out of twelve jurors agree. If the jury can't agree to convict or acquit, a mistrial is declared, which means the trial will have to be held again with a new jury. If the jury can't agree, this is also known as a hung jury).

Instructions to the Judge: You are in charge of the trial. You may refer to a lawyer as "counsel." You must rule on any objections by the attorneys. If you agree with an objection, you say, "Objection sustained." If you disagree with the objection, you give your reasons and say, "Objection overruled." Witnesses first receive a "direct examination" by the first attorney and then a "cross-exam" by the other attorney. You may allow redirect or recross-examination if time permits and the attorneys need it. After both sides have rested their cases, the attorneys give closing arguments, and the jury is given the above instructions by the judge.

*Note: Although criminal defendants may not be forced to testify, if they do decide to testify at trial, they must submit to cross-examination by the prosecutor.

The jury deliberates. After the jury reaches a decision, the bailiff is informed and the jury is brought back into court. The judge asks if they have reached a decision and, if so, who speaks for the jury? The foreperson speaks. Then the judge asks what the jury's verdict is. The foreperson tells the court. If "guilty," the judge must pronounce sentence. If the verdict is "not guilty," the judge announces that the Defendant has been *acquitted* and is free to go.

The judge is responsible for conducting the trial and keeping order in the court. If an attorney, witness or bystander is rude or fails to heed the judge's order, the judge would say, "You are in contempt of court." The judge may assess a fine and/or have the person in contempt removed from the courtroom by the bailiff.

Cue Cards

The Prosecutor must ask the right questions to elicit the facts from the witnesses in order to prove the case. He must prove all the facts of the case beyond a reasonable doubt. An example of a necessary fact would be: Betsy must identify Stella as the robber.

The Defense Attorney must try to show that no crime took place. Perhaps Stella Strongarm was just joking or Betsy really volunteered to give Stella the money and now wants it back, or perhaps it was someone who looked like Stella Strongarm who robbed Betsy Bystander.

Witness for the Defense. You think that you saw Stella at the movies at the time the crime supposedly occurred. You aren't completely sure since it was dark in the theater. But you are a friend of Stella's and would like to help her out. However, you are not willing to lie.

Witness for the Prosecution. You were standing across the hall when Betsy gave Stella the money. You aren't friends with either girl. You couldn't hear what happened, but you think Betsy looked scared and Stella looked threatening. You definitely saw Betsy give the money to Stella.

Police Officer—Witness for the Prosecution. You took the complaint from Betsy. You interviewed the witness for the prosecution. You did not speak to the defense witness. Most of your testimony is hearsay.

Objections. (A copy of this cue card should be given to both attorneys and the judge.)

While your opposing counsel is questioning witnesses, you may "object" if you think that a question is improper for one or more of the following reasons by saying,

"Your, Honor, I object to the question because it is (pick one or more):

a. *irrelevant*

b. asking for *hearsay* (asks for an answer not in the direct knowledge of the witness)

c. *leading* (it gives the witness a hint by giving the answer within the question
Note: Leading questions are acceptable and may be asked on "cross-examination," but not on "direct examination." (Attorneys *directly* examine [question] their own "friendly" witnesses and "cross-examine" the opposition's "unfriendly" witnesses.)

The judge rules on the objections. If the judge agrees with the objection, he will say, "Objection sustained." If he does not agree, he will say, "Objection overruled," and the witness may answer the question.

Case of the Forged Working Papers

Case of the Forged Working Papers

Gracie Gogetter was fifteen. She decided to answer an ad in a local newspaper and get a newspaper route. She went to the local office of the *Daily Bugle* and applied. She was told that because she was under eighteen she would need to have a work permit signed by her parents. Gracie was excited. She would easily be able to make $20 a week delivering papers.

> **Gracie's mom took away all of her earnings.**

Because she was in a hurry, Gracie did not take the work permit all the way home. Instead of having her mother or father sign it, Gracie signed it herself, with her mother's name.

Gracie took the permit back to the newspaper office. They hardly looked at the signature, but they did assign Gracie a paper route on the spot. She began delivering the paper conscientiously after school that week. After a few weeks of delivering the newspaper, Gracie's mom noticed that she had much more money than she received for her allowance.

"Oh, didn't I tell you, Mom? I got a paper route delivering the *Daily Bugle*!" said Gracie.

"I'm sorry, Gracie," her mother replied. "Your grades in school are poor enough as it is. I don't want you using homework time delivering papers. And besides that, I'm going to complain to the newspaper because they let you work without my permission!"

Mrs. Gogetter called the *Daily Bugle* office. After a brief conversation, she put down the phone, turned, and angrily gave Gracie a hard slap. Furthermore, her mother took away all Gracie's earnings and put them in a bank account maintained for Gracie's college education.

What's Your Opinion?

What's Your Opinion?

1. Can Gracie's mother take away money that Gracie earned from the paper route?

The Law Says:

Yes. Until you reach the age of majority (legal adulthood) which is 18 in most states, parents have the right to control your finances—even money you have earned yourself. However, parents also have the legal responsibility to financially support their children as well, supplying all their basic needs for food, shelter, clothing and medical care.

What's Your Opinion?

2. Can Gracie's mother slap her or ground her for such a minor offense?

The Law Says:

Yes. Parents have a right to use a "reasonable" amount of force or corporal punishment to discipline their children and regulate their behavior.

What's Your Opinion?

3. Was the station manager of the *Daily Bugle* guilty of breaking the law?

The Law Says:

No, not unless he had a reason to know that Mrs. Gogetter's signature was forged. If he knew it was a forgery, he would be guilty of violation of the state's labor laws.

What If?

1. **What If** Gracie's mother had given her permission to work? Could she still take Gracie's earnings?

   Answer: Yes. Since Gracie's parents have the responsibility of supporting her until she reaches the age of majority (eighteen), they are also entitled to control any wages she makes until that time.

2. **What If** Gracie's mother told Gracie's dad and he was so furious that he whipped her with his belt until she had bruises all over her body? Is that a crime?

   Answer: Yes. Even parents cannot inflict excessive discipline on their children. Serious beatings that raise welts or make bruises or are frequent or severe cross into the area of "child abuse."

3. **What If** Gracie's parents were guilty of discipline which was too extreme? What could Gracie do?

   Answer: Gracie could tell her schoolteacher, counselor, the police, or call the state agency responsible for the protection of children. These people can and will help. They are required by law to assist and protect children in danger. No one deserves that kind of treatment.

Activities

1. Since the rules which govern child labor vary from state to state, write to your State Labor Department to find out what you would need to do in order to be employed. What do you think the regulations should include?

2. To understand the need for child labor laws, do some research on the history of the factory system in this country and in England. During the Industrial Revolution in the eighteenth, nineteenth and early twentieth centuries, children as young as five years old worked in coal mines, textile mills, tobacco factories and many other industries. These children, who were not given an education, were virtual captives of an economic system which crowded them into dangerous, unsanitary factories and worked them ten to sixteen hours a day.

   How could it happen that the laws in England and then in America permitted this to take place and justified it as well? What kinds of attitudes existed in our country before 1938 when the Wages and Hours Act was finally passed? It was this act that is now the basic child labor law for the United States. Prepare a group report on this gruesome and shameful chapter in history. Research child labor abuses existing today in other parts of the world.

3. You are a state legislator. Write a law and/or argue for a law to regulate child labor. Specify the kinds of work children under 18 can or cannot do. Include limits on hours they can work, weights they can lift and specific jobs that are too dangerous, dirty or otherwise unfit. Also include a provision for minimum wages. How would you make your laws enforceable? What kinds of penalties would you impose on employers who violated your law?

   Role Play Alternative: "Congress is now in session." Take versions of the laws written above and have the class debate them as if each student was a legislator from a different area. Some legislators represent farm areas, some industrial areas. Have some discuss lowering the minimum wage for people under 18. Create compromise legislation until one version finally passes by a majority vote.

4. As a young employee you are entitled to Social Security benefits if you are disabled, unemployment compensation if you are laid off, and worker's compensation if you are injured on the job. One of the first items you must attend to is obtaining your Social Security number, which you will have for your entire life. Locate your Social Security Administration Office in your phone book under United States Government. Write to them or visit the office with your parents for information on how to obtain your Social Security number.

Case of the Poor Divorced Parent

Case of the Poor Divorced Parents

Max and Sara Stalwart were married and had two children—Junior, nine, and Missy, twelve. Max was a rock and roll musician and Sara was a nurse. Max worked at different "gigs" all over the country, and Sara worked at a nearby hospital.

Mom and Dad weren't getting along too well. Max was so often away from home that Sara felt he wasn't able to do his share in the marriage. Max was, however, trying hard to make a living as a musician, which was his only skill.

> **The judge ordered Max to pay child support.**

Unable to reconcile their differences, Sara filed for a divorce in the state court. Max was sad but didn't contest the divorce. Sara asked the court for custody of Junior and Missy. Max agreed. Junior thought he'd rather travel around with his dad than live with his mom, but no one asked about his preference.

On the day of the court hearing, the judge granted the divorce and awarded custody of Junior and Missy to their mom. The judge ordered Max to give Sara money each month for child support. The amount of support was based on Max and Sara's incomes with a formula determined by the state. The judge gave Max the right to visit the children or have them visit him once a week and on some holidays.

Unfortunately, Max often failed to give Sara the money for child support. Sara still worked at the hospital, but without money from Max, it was hard to make ends meet.

What's Your Opinion?

What's Your Opinion?

1. Should the judge ask the children which parent they would prefer to live with? Should the children's preferences be the determining factor for the court to use when deciding custody?

The Law Says:

If the parents have already decided between them which parent will get custody of the children, the courts will likely honor the parents' decision. If the parents cannot decide themselves and are battling over custody of the children, some judges will ask the children what their preferences are, especially if the children are older. In contested cases, the final decision will be made by the judge.

What's Your Opinion?

2. What standards or guidelines should a judge use when deciding which parent should get custody of the children?

The Law Says:

The law is very clear that the judge must decide based upon "the best interest of the child." This would include which parent can provide the most stable environment, which situation would cause the least disruption in the lives of the children and which parent can take the best care of the children. However, the judge should not consider which parent makes the most money when making the decision.

What's Your Opinion?

3. Isn't it possible that the parents could share custody even though the parents are not living together after the divorce?

The Law Says:

Yes, it is possible that the children could alternate for more or less equal periods of time between the parents. Courts are increasingly accepting this arrangement known legally as "joint custody." Usually the children go back and forth between the parents' homes, but sometimes the children stay in one home and the parents alternate living there.

What's Your Opinion?

4. Is there anywhere Sara's family can seek assistance since they can't make ends meet on her salary alone?

The Law Says:

Yes. If there is a need for help, all states have assistance programs called Aid to Families with Dependent Children (AFDC or ADC). To qualify, there are certain income guidelines and a certain amount of paperwork, but local welfare or social service officials can often help speed up the process—especially in emergencies.

What's Your Opinion?

5. Will the government help Sara collect child support from Max? How?

The Law Says:

Yes. All states have mechanisms for enforcing support orders when the "non-custodial" parent fails to pay. In many states an agency called the Friend of the Court or a similar agency will automatically begin collection procedures against the nonpaying parent. However, it is always helpful for the custodial parent (Sara, in this case) to call that agency and make sure they know about the problem and begin to act. Although the children live with their mother, the father is equally responsible under the law for the support of his children until they reach eighteen years of age.

What If?

1. **What If** Max loses his job? Is he still responsible for child support?

    Answer: Yes. Although losing a job is serious, so is the responsibility for child support. Courts will sometimes reduce the amount of monthly support payments if a parent loses a job or takes a job at a lower salary. But the court will not go below a certain minimum amount. The court may also allow the parent to delay support payments until he gets a new job, but he must ultimately pay the "arrearage" (the amount that he falls behind).

2. **What If** Sara remarries? Is Max still responsible for child support, even if Sara's new husband is very rich?

    Answer: Yes. Unless Sara's new husband legally adopts Junior and Missy and assumes responsibility for their support, Max is still responsible. The new husband could only adopt the children if Max agreed to the adoption.

3. **What If** your parents are divorced and your noncustodial parent comes to pick you up unexpectedly from home or school? You suspect that your custodial parent has not consented to this visit and you feel uncomfortable. What should you do?

    Answer: If you have any doubts about going with your parent at that time, try to inform your custodial parent. If you are in school, tell your teacher or principal and ask him/her to contact your other parent. Do not leave before permission is granted and everyone is sure the plan is OK.

Activities

1. Having children is a responsibility for the parents which involves a lifetime commitment of love and caring. The human baby is the most helpless and dependent of all the mammals. This relationship of child dependency and parental responsibility is cleverly demonstrated by a school lesson which was devised to emphasize the rigors of parenting*. We will call it "The Coddling of Baby Egg." Each student will care for a raw egg as if it were an infant, for one week. The teacher will sign each egg to guarantee there will be no substitutions in case of mishaps or "child" abuse. The students must make a crib or carrier for the egg and take it with them everywhere. The "infants" must be cared for twenty-four hours a day,

*Irwin, Jim, *Detroit Free Press*, June 5, 1986, Section 2A, "A class full of good eggs," Macomb North Section. Cited with permission.

as in real life. If the "parent" absolutely can't take the "infant" with him or her, then a dependable "egg-sitter" must be found who will take the chore seriously. "Baby" may be dressed and made to look like the real thing. No fair if you hard-boil the "Baby." (The teacher will break the eggs at the end of the week to check.) During the project keep a journal of your experiences. After the project, write a reflective paper on the fragility, the inconvenience, and the interminable burden of care "Baby Egg" required. What can you conclude from this about authentic child care?

2. Research the names of human service agencies in your city, county, or state which are responsible for the welfare of children. These may be private, public, or religious social agencies which help families and minor children. One place to look is in the Yellow Pages of your phone directory under Social Service Organizations.

3. Check your library for *The Boys and Girls Book About Divorce*, by Richard A. Gardner, copyright 1983, Jason Aranson Publishers, New York. This book is written for children and recommended by Parents Without Partners, an organization for single parents. Another valuable divorce book was written by twenty students (ages 11-14): *The Kids Book of Divorce: By, for & About Kids*, edited by their teacher, Eric Rofes, copyright 1982, Vintage Books, New York.

4. List on the chalkboard reasons for the following: How is a marriage a legal contract? (**Answer:** Contracts require that the parties exchange one thing of value for another. In marriage, the parties exchange vows [promises]. They promise to love, honor and cherish each other.) Do you think that these promises are valuable enough to form the basis of a contract?

5. Marriage is different from any other contract. Can you list the ways that it is different? (**Answer:** 1. It requires a license issued by the state before the parties can enter into it. Most other contracts do not require state approval or licenses. 2. If the parties want to end a marriage contract, the state court must supervise the divorce. Other contracts can be ended by mutual consent of the parties, without government approval.)

Case of the Graffiti Artist

Vandalism/Malicious Destruction of Property

Case of the Graffiti Artist

Rebecca Rembrandt and Sammy Cezanne, two aspiring neighborhood artists, wanted to create a chalk masterpiece on Sammy's driveway. With permission from Sammy's mom, they were soon hard at work with plenty of chalk, transforming their big concrete "canvas" into a work of art. After a little while, Rebecca got bored with the driveway and decided to move on to bigger and better things. She found a can of red spray paint and headed to the school across the street. Overcome with inspiration, she spray painted the school with the words "So many walls. So little time."

> **Overcome with inspiration, she spray painted the school wall.**

Just as she was finishing, a police car pulled up. The police detained Rembrandt and told her she was under arrest for "malicious destruction of property."

But I didn't destroy anything!" she protested. "And if this is a crime, then I'm not the only one who's a criminal. Look what Sammy Cezanne drew on the driveway."

The police went over and looked at the chalk drawing on Sammy's driveway.

"Did you do this?" one of the policemen asked Sammy.

He didn't know how to respond. "I, uhh, umm, I . . . ."

"Where do you live?" the officer interrupted Sammy's stuttering.

The boy pointed to his house—next to the drive. The police noted that the writing on the sidewalk was chalk and not paint. They did not arrest Sammy, but they promptly took Rebecca Rembrandt down to the station and called her parents.

What's Your Opinion?

What's Your Opinion?

1. How would you define *vandalism*?

The Law Says:

Vandalism is the intentional destruction, damaging, or defacing of someone else's property. Legally, vandalism is called "malicious destruction of property" or "malicious mischief." The crime may be either a misdemeanor or a felony depending upon the amount of damage.

What's Your Opinion?

2. Why did the police decide that painting on the school wall was a crime but writing on the driveway was not?

The Law Says:

The chalk used on the sidewalk was not permanent and it would wash away in the rain. Paint, however, must be cleaned off the wall. Spray paint would have to be removed by the school custodian and would take hours of work and the use of cleaning compounds. Since the school district would have to pay the custodian to remove the graffiti, the spray paint prank was costly.

Sammy Cezanne drew the chalk pattern on his own property. A home owner has the right to alter his or her property in this way.

What's Your Opinion?

3. Is the breaking of windows in an abandoned house malicious destruction of property, even though no one lives there? Why?

The Law Says:

Yes. That the house is abandoned makes no difference. The house is still someone else's property. The owner may be planning to sell it, to rehabilitate it or move back in.

What If?

1. **What If** Rebecca Rembrandt had written on the school wall in chalk instead of paint? Would that have made a difference?

   Answer: This is not such a clear case of vandalism since chalk can eventually wear off the school wall. But the school principal might decide to have the custodian wash the chalk off the surfaces because it defaced the school. In that case the time and money spent cleaning would be considered "damages" in a legal sense and could be prosecuted.

2. **What If** either Rebecca Rembrandt or Sammy Cezanne had drawn in chalk on a neighbor's sidewalk? Is that a crime?

   Answer: The practical answer is that one must always ask permission of a property owner before doing anything that might be objectionable. Never assume that it is all right to post signs or draw pictures on any property that is not your own. If the neighbor objects to the "art," the artist could be prosecuted.

Activities

1. What are the costs of vandalism to society? And who pays?

2. Would your attitude be affected, as a law-abiding citizen, if the graffiti made a political statement with which you agreed?

3. What is the difference between harmless pranks and vandalism on Halloween?

4. Write an editorial which protests malicious destruction of property and calls for a legal solution.

5. Look up the word *vandal* in the dictionary. What are its historic origins? (Also look up *Hun* and *Attila*.)

6. List all of the consequences of breaking a one dollar window in an empty house in the middle of winter. (**Answer:** The cold air could freeze the pipes and cause them to burst and flood the house. The water could short out the electrical system and cause a fire. Animals could get in through the broken window and cause havoc. Breaking a one dollar window could cause the destruction of an entire house!)

Case of the Green Armbands

Freedom of Speech/Freedom of Expression

Case of the Green Armbands

A group of students in the Civics Club at Patrick Henry Middle School were concerned about the United States' involvement in the nuclear arms race. To show their support for peace and nuclear disarmament, they decided to attend school for one week wearing green armbands. Hearing of the plan, and fearing that school would be disrupted, the principal, Ms. Gladys Grimm, made a rule against wearing armbands. In spite of the rule, some students came to school wearing armbands anyway. The students were suspended and sued the school district in federal court for violating their First Amendment rights.

> **The students sued the school district for violating their First Amendment rights.**

What's Your Opinion?

What's Your Opinion?

1. Read the Preamble to the U.S. Constitution and then read the First Amendment. (Both are in the Appendix.) List the freedoms guaranteed by the First Amendment. Why do you think that the authors of the Constitution considered those freedoms to be so important and fundamental? Why was it necessary to guarantee them in the highest law of the land?

The Law Says:

The framers of the Constitution believed that these freedoms were absolutely necessary to "secure the blessings of liberty." To be truly free, those freedoms are fundamental. The thirteen colonies had just freed themselves from the tyranny of King George and the British Empire. The authors of the Constitution knew, firsthand, that the people must retain those rights, by law, to guarantee that the government could never deny those rights to the people.

What's Your Opinion?

2. Who will win the case—the students or the principal? Why?

The Law Says:

The students will win. This case is based on an actual case that was eventually decided by the U.S. Supreme Court in *Tinker vs. Des Moines School District* 393 U.S. 503 (1969). The plaintiffs were John Tinker, 15; Mary Beth Tinker, 13; and Christopher Eckhardt, 15—all who opposed the participation of the United States in the Vietnam War. They were sent home from school after wearing black armbands to express their opposition to the Vietnam War. A lower federal court decided in favor of the principal. The students appealed and the Supreme Court, the highest court in the United States, reversed the decision of the lower court and ruled in favor of the students. The Supreme Court said that wearing armbands was protected under the First Amendment to the Constitution, which guarantees freedom of speech. The court called the wearing of armbands "'symbolic' speech." The court ruled that school officials could not prohibit such speech if the prohibition was merely to avoid peaceful discussion of legitimate topics of debate. Nor could the principal prohibit such a demonstration because of the vague fear that it *might* disrupt school. A mere possibility of disruption is not enough to deprive people of their rights to free speech. The principal could restrict a display only if one or more of the following conditions were true: (a) The display would *certainly* disrupt the operation of the school. (b) The protest would infringe on other people's rights.

What's Your Opinion?

3. Would it be proper for the principal to allow the wearing of political paraphernalia, buttons, bumper stickers, etc., only in the cafeteria during lunch hours but not allow it anywhere else in the school at any time?

The Law Says:

Perhaps. *Reasonable* rules can restrict the *time*, *manner* and *place* of free speech as long as the regulations do not apply to the subject matter if the reason for the rules is "compelling." For example, it would be legitimate for a city to make an ordinance prohibiting use of loudspeakers from 9 p.m. to 9 a.m. on city streets. It would not be legitimate to allow loudspeakers only to advertise one political party but prohibit it for another (TIME: 9 p.m.—9 a.m.; MANNER: loudspeaker; PLACE: city streets).

What's Your Opinion?

4. Do you think the *Tinker* case applies to all public schools? Why or why not?

The Law Says:

Yes. Since the *Tinker* case was decided by the U.S. Supreme Court, the decision applies to all public schools in the United States. Private schools are not included in the *Tinker* decision because attendance at private schools is voluntary while attendance at public schools is mandatory.

What's Your Opinion?

5. Reread the First Amendment. This amendment guarantees freedom of religion to everyone. But it also prohibits the government from establishing any state-sponsored religion. Given that there is freedom of religion, if a student chooses to make a brief, private prayer in school, before class starts, can he or she do so?

The Law Says:

Yes. The government cannot interfere with the free exercise of religion unless there is an overwhelming reason.* On the other hand, the school or teacher cannot require or request, or even suggest, that students make any prayer, even if the prayer is completely optional. The courts have ruled that even optional prayers put impermissible pressure on students to conform and therefore violate the "establishment" clause of the Constitution. (The "establishment clause" is the clause that forbids the government from establishing an official religion.)

*compelling state interest

What If?

1. **What If** the people wearing the armbands blocked the doors to the school and other students were not able to enter? Would that be permissible?

   Answer: No. The second part of the Supreme Court test was that protestors may not interfere with the freedom of other people who are not participating. Blocking the entrance would be improper.

2. **What If** the principal allowed students to wear armbands but prohibited them from wearing buttons with political slogans, peace signs, and witty sayings? Would this be valid prohibition?

   Answer: No. Though only armbands were the explicit subject in the *Tinker* case, all other forms of nondisruptive expression were clearly included in the decision.

3. **What If** instead of protesting nuclear war, the students wanted to wear swastikas to show their support for Hitler and his Nazi party? Could that be prohibited by the principal?

   Answer: No. As long as the demonstration was peaceful and not disruptive, even very unpopular opinions have the right to be expressed. This is difficult for many people to accept. Freedom of speech must extend to all opinions, both popular and unpopular, if we are to be truly free.

Activities

1. Post the First Amendment for the class. Brainstorm the following: Imagine what might happen if the First Amendment did not exist. Think about the abuses of government power that could result.

2. Have a town meeting. Include people who support the position that school is not the place for political expression. Also include those who feel that students are citizens who have the right to express themselves on important issues, in appropriate ways, in school. Keep in mind that a principal must balance the rights of students and teachers to express themselves freely, with the need to maintain an effective educational environment. There is a sensitive balance between one person's right to free speech and another person's right to an orderly classroom where learning can take place.

3. In the *Tinker* case, Justice Fortas, writing for the majority of the Supreme Court, wrote:

   > Unless it is proven that the expression of opinion will create a substantial interference with school work or discipline, students are entitled to freedom of expression of their views.

   Is it possible that people will have different views of exactly what this means? With a partner, give some examples of what you think is an acceptable or unacceptable expression of opinion in a school setting. Is "substantial interference with school" easy or hard to define?

4. **You Be the Judge:** You are a municipal judge in the city of Anytown. Mr. Jerry Joker is brought before you by the Anytown Prosecuting Attorney. Mr. Joker is charged with a misdemeanor called "Reckless Endangerment," because he allegedly yelled out "Fire," in a crowded movie theater as a prank. Several people were hurt in the panic that followed as they rushed to escape even though there was actually no fire.

At the trial, Mr. Joker admits he yelled "Fire," as a prank. But Mr. Joker and his attorney claim that the law is invalid. They claim the law of "Reckless Endangerment" is unconstitutional because it deprives Mr. Joker of his First Amendment right to freedom of speech. Joker and his attorney also say the law is vague and too broad.

The Prosecuting Attorney notes that even free speech has its limits—especially where it endangers public safety.

As judge, you know that the U.S. Supreme Court has ruled that freedom of speech is called a "fundamental right." But the Supreme Court has also said that even "fundamental rights" may be limited where there is a "compelling state interest" (a matter of overriding importance which requires government intervention).

The "Reckless Endangerment" statute (law) reads as follows: "Anyone who shall incite a group of people to panic or riot by use of inflammatory or false statements shall be guilty of a misdemeanor punishable by not more than six months in jail and/or a $500 fine."

You be the judge. Write a legal opinion ruling on the constitutionality of the law. Is there a "compelling state interest" here? Also respond to Mr. Joker's argument that the law is vague and too broad.

5. **Bonus Question:** The First Amendment to the Constitution says: "Congress shall make no law . . . abridging the freedom of speech." The amendment refers only to the U.S. Congress. It does not say *states* cannot make such laws. The school district in the *Tinker* case was a state school in Iowa. Why did the Supreme Court decide that the First Amendment applied to states, too? (**Answer:** The Fourteenth Amendment reads, in part, "No State shall make or enforce any law which shall abridge the privileges or immunities of citizens of the United States . . . ." This makes all of the guarantees of the Constitution apply to state as well as federal government.)

Case of the Cafeteria Food Fight

Disorderly Conduct

Case of the Cafeteria Food Fight

It all started in Mom & Pop's Restaurant when Ada Gourmet tossed a few fries in the air at lunchtime to show her friends how she could catch each one in her mouth like a trained seal.

"Here. Toss one here," shouted an enthusiast from the next table.

Ada threw a couple of fries eight feet away. Everything was all right until one of the potato missiles found its way into Richie Buber's hair,

> **When it was all over, Norman Nebish had an injured eye.**

which he definitely did not appreciate. He whipped an apple back to Ada's camp. Predictably, the apple caught somebody on the cheek, and the hostilities soon escalated into a full blown food war. The apple made the rounds for two minutes.

When the battle was brought under control by Mom and Pop (the owners), Norman Nebish was covering his injured eye and the floor looked like a war zone. Later, it was learned that Norman was taken to Anytown Hospital's emergency room. There was concern over his impaired vision.

What's Your Opinion?

What's Your Opinion?

1. Do you think that any crimes were committed by the students? If so, can you name them?

The Law Says:

Yes. Most obviously, the students committed the misdemeanor of "disorderly conduct," also known as "disturbing the peace." Another crime here might be "malicious destruction of property" if the fight caused any damage. (See "Case of the Graffiti Artist.") It is also possible that the person who hit Norman Nebish with the apple could be guilty of assault and battery if it was done *intentionally.*

What's Your Opinion?

2. Who might be held civilly responsible for the injury to Norman Nebish? Why?

The Law Says:

It is possible that everyone who participated in the food fight could be held responsible! This would happen if a judge or jury decided that the participants caused Norman's injury by their *negligence. Negligence* means that they neglected their duty to behave responsibly.

Certainly whoever threw the apple could be held responsible. The problem is proving exactly who threw it. Ada Gourmet would be a likely target of a lawsuit since she was the instigator, as would Richie Buber, who first tossed the apple. Even the owners of the restaurant could be held responsible if it is shown that they did not do enough to control their student patrons.

What If?

1. **What If** a motorist driving by the restaurant sees the food fight in progress inside? He is so distracted that he hits a telephone pole. Later, he also files a lawsuit against Pop, Ada Gourmet and Richie Buber. Do you think he would win?

   Answer: Not likely. The *actual cause* of his accident was not really the food fight, but rather the driver's own fault in not paying attention to his driving.

2. **What If** the participants are found guilty of disorderly conduct, or disturbing the peace or malicious destruction of property? Could a judge, as part of the "sentence" (punishment), make the guilty students pay for cleaning or repairing the restaurant?

Answer: Yes. Very often in cases where damages are done, a judge will make the convicted party pay for repairs. This is known as "restitution." Some judges may also make people convicted of minor crimes do community service work.

Activities

1. Role-play a teacher or administrator who walks into the school lunchroom where a food fight was just beginning. You are concerned about the possibility of injury occurring to the students. What would you do to bring order to this mess? Later, as you think about it, how could such a scene be avoided in the future? Could schedules, lunchroom rules, or other strategies be used to prevent trouble?

2. **You Be the Judge:** Role-play this case.
   The case: *Norman Nebish, Plaintiff, vs. Mom & Pop's Restaurant, Richie Buber, and Ada Gourmet, Defendants.*

   You are the judge presiding over this civil case. At the trial, several witnesses testified to seeing Richie throw the apple that hit Norman. Richie Buber admitted that just before throwing the apple, he said, "Let's see if I can turn Norman's noodle into apple strudel."

   Witnesses also testified that Mom and Pop, owners of the restaurant, had tried hard to stop the food fight and that Ada Gourmet had started it with her French fry antics. This is a civil case with Norman Nebish suing all of the defendants for his hospital and doctor bills and for missing several days of work due to a headache.

   You must decide which, if any, of the defendants must pay for Norman Nebish's injuries and why. (**Hint:** Since Mom and Pop tried to stop the fight, they are not likely to be held responsible. Richie Buber is obviously in trouble. A judge or jury could go either way concerning Ada. She may be responsible for starting the food fight, but her actions may be too remote to be considered a "proximate," or actual, cause of Norman's injury.)

3. Write a response to the following question regarding this case. Would it make a difference to you, as the judge, if Norman Nebish, who claims the cafeteria fight caused him to have a terrible headache, had previously complained of a bad headache a week before the fight? Explain.

4. Explain how people act differently in crowds than they do as individuals. Why do you think this is so? (**Answer:** Anonymity plays a part; diffusion of responsibility helps create the mob mentality.)

Case of the Shortcut Caper

Private Property/ Trespassing

Case of the Shortcut Caper

As usual, Willie Walker was in a hurry to get to the Anytown Shopping Mall after school. He knew he could save at least ten minutes by cutting through the Baskerville's backyard. Willie didn't know that the Baskerville family had just bought a really nasty watchdog. The Baskerville house had been burglarized and they wanted a dog to protect their property! Carefree—Willie leaped the fence into the waiting jaws of Fang, the hound of the Basker-villes. Willie barely escaped becoming Fang's afternoon snack! He threw himself back over the fence with the dog's jaws firmly attached to his sneaker. His heart pounded against his chest as he finally escaped Fang's fearsome choppers. Willie's jeans were shredded, he lost one sneaker, and he was scared out of his mind.

Willie thought he'd save ten minutes.

What's Your Opinion?

What's Your Opinion?

1. How would you define *trespassing*?

The Law Says:

Trespassing is entry onto or interference with the property of another person without permission. It can be both a civil and a criminal violation.

What's Your Opinion?

2. Can Willie Walker sue the Baskervilles?

The Law Says:

This is a trick question. Yes, Willie can sue. But will he win? Not likely. He is a trespasser and has very few legal rights in this situation.

What's Your Opinion?

3. Does it make a difference that the Baskervilles had a fence around their property?

The Law Says:

Yes. The fence makes it clear that the owners do not want people coming onto their property.

What's Your Opinion?

4. Shouldn't the Baskervilles have posted a sign saying, "No Trespassing" or "Beware of Dog"?

The Law Says:

Not in this case. If the family did not have a fence around their lot and it wasn't clearly private property, then a sign would be necessary to inform others.

What If?

1. **What If** Fang attacked the newspaper carrier who was delivering the paper to the front door? Would the Baskervilles be liable then?

Answer: Probably. Especially if Fang had a history of biting people or being vicious. The laws used to be that a dog would get "one free bite," before the owner became liable for its bites. The theory was that until the owner had reason to know the dog bit people, he wasn't negligent. Today most states hold dog owners to a higher level of responsibility for their pets' behavior. Also, in this case, the newspaper carrier was "invited" by the Baskervilles to deliver the paper. When you invite someone onto your property, you have a higher level of responsibility for their safety than you have to a trespasser.

2. **What If** a guest slips and falls on the Baskervilles' icy steps? Who would be responsible for the injuries?

Answer: The Baskervilles would be liable. Property owners have a legal *duty* to maintain their premises in a reasonably safe condition for the benefit of legitimate guests. Cleaning ice and snow from porches and walks is part of that duty in most states.

3. **What If** the Baskervilles tear down their fence and build a swimming pool in the backyard? One day some neighboring children sneak into the pool and one drowns. Would the Baskervilles be liable for the death of the child?

Answer: Yes, very likely—especially since they had removed the fence around their property. Things like swimming pools, large piles of dirt and discarded refrigerators are known as "attractive nuisances." The law recognizes that owners have special responsibilities to stop neighborhood children from being attracted to such dangerous areas.

Activities

1. There is a tree in a neighbor's yard on the way home from school which is laden with big, luscious apples. The owner never seems to pick them and many are left to fall and rot on the ground. Nobody really seems to care one way or the other. Since the fruit is going to waste anyway, do you think you could help yourself to an apple by putting your arm through the fence? You wouldn't even have to go into the yard to get the fruit. Is this trespassing? Or is it something else? Write a paragraph that expresses your view of this? (**Answer:** Reaching through the fence, if your arm crosses over the property line, is a trespass. Taking the apples, like picking a flower, is also larceny [theft]. If the property owner complains to the police, you could be in trouble.)

2. **Role Play:** If you were a defense attorney, how would you defend your apple picking client on the basis that the property owner didn't seem to want the fruit? Prepare a convincing case for the court. If you were the prosecutor, what arguments would you make?

3. **You Be the Judge:** One dark midnight, Gertie Goofer breaks into a vacant house owned by Harry Hostile. Because the house has been repeatedly ransacked, Mr. Hostile has set up a booby trap. When Gertie enters the front door, she trips a wire connected to the trigger of a shotgun. The gun goes off, severely wounding Gertie. After getting out of the hospital, Gertie is tried and convicted of "breaking and entering." This does not stop her from suing Mr. Hostile for the injuries caused by his booby trap.

The case comes before you. You must find for or against Gertie in the civil lawsuit for damages. Write the decision in the case of *Gertie Goofer vs. Harry Hostile*. Justify your decision. (**Answer:** Mr. Hostile would be found liable for Gertie's injuries and would have to pay for her hospital bills, at least. The logic: Shooting someone for breaking into a vacant house is considered excessive force since it exceeds the punishment that the law allows. It might be a different matter if Mr. Hostile was in the house and thought his life was being threatened by a burglar. Refer to the assault and battery case.)

4. Can you think of situations when necessity would be a defense for trespassing? Describe such emergencies in a brainstorming session.

5. How would you feel if it were permissible for anyone to walk on your property at any time? List the reasons why you think "No Trespassing" laws are important. (**Answer:** To ensure personal privacy; to avoid the possibility that someone may be injured on your property for which you may have to pay; to guarantee the benefits of private property.)

Case of the Truant School Ghouls

Truancy

Case of the Truant School Ghouls

A bunch of students at Anytown Middle School formed a club called the Ghouls. One beautiful spring day the Ghouls decided they would much rather play video games than be in school. In between classes they all slipped out a rear door when no one was watching and headed uptown.

While they were hanging out in Duke's Video Arcade, Officer Eagle-Eyes spotted them. He knew it was a school day and came up to ask them why they weren't in class. Big Wilbur Windbag, the leader of the Ghouls, stepped forward.

> **Officer Eagle-Eyes was not convinced.**

"Our teacher was sick and they couldn't get a substitute or anything, so class was dismissed early." He was very sincere.

Officer Eagle-Eyes was not convinced. He decided to take all five Ghouls into "custody" even though he wasn't sure that Wilbur's story was a lie. He took them back to school and into the office where the principal, Ms. Ruth Ruler, was extremely happy to see all of the Ghouls.

What's Your Opinion?

What's Your Opinion?

1. What is an arrest?

The Law Says:

An arrest is the lawful deprivation of freedom to leave. One is under arrest if one is detained involuntarily or taken into custody.

What's Your Opinion?

2. How do you know if you are under arrest?

The Law Says:

A police officer should tell you. If you are not sure, ask, "Am I under arrest?"

What's Your Opinion?

3. Can a police officer take a minor into custody even if the officer is not sure that the minor has committed a crime? Under what circumstances?

The Law Says:

Yes. Although it is not a formal arrest, most states allow police officers to take juveniles into "protective custody" if they have reason to believe that the minor is "in need of supervision," has run away from home, is skipping school or is in a dangerous situation. This is not a formal arrest, but it is effectively the same thing, except the police cannot legally search a minor in protective custody.

What's Your Opinion?

4. If a minor is arrested or taken into custody, what must the police officer do as soon as possible?

The Law Says:

The police must call the minor's parents as soon as possible. In this case, returning the students to the custody of the principal is probably an acceptable alternative since school officials are considered to be "in loco parentis," (the legal equivalent to parents during school hours).

What's Your Opinion?

5. Could a police officer arrest or take an adult into custody if no crime was committed? Explain.

The Law Says:

No. A police officer cannot arrest (or search) an adult unless the officer has an arrest warrant or search warrant signed by a judge or if the officer has "probable cause" to believe that a felony was committed and that the person about to be arrested committed it. (See also "Case of the Forgotten Fudge" and reread the Fourth Amendment to the *Constitution*.)

What's Your Opinion?
6. How would you define *juvenile delinquent?*

The Law Says:
A juvenile delinquent is a minor who has committed a crime or violated the law. Juveniles who have not committed crimes but are having serious behavior problems, such as truancy or running away from home, are known as "minors in need of supervision" or M.I.N.S.

What's Your Opinion?
7. Who finally decides if a juvenile is delinquent or in need of supervision?

The Law Says:
A special juvenile court judge, referee or jury would hold a hearing or trial to decide. Such a decision requires "due process" to safeguard the rights of minors.

What's Your Opinion?
8. What punishment could the Ghouls receive for cutting class?

The Law Says:
If this was their first "offense," the principal would decide on a fair punishment, such as extra work, suspension, or "detention hours" before or after school. If the Ghouls repeatedly cut class, they could be tried in juvenile court and possibly be sent away to special schools for delinquent minors until they reach legal adulthood.

What If?

1. **What If** school had really been dismissed early and Wilbur Windbag had been telling the truth? Would Officer Eagle-Eyes be in trouble for his actions?

   Answer: Probably not. The standard for taking juveniles into custody is so broad that it gives police a large amount of discretion for such behavior. As long as the officer acted reasonably under the circumstances, the officer would probably be immune from legal action.

2. **What If** the officer searched one of the Ghouls and found a bag of marijuana? Would he be able to charge the student with possession of drugs?

   Answer: Such a charge would probably not hold up unless the officer had "probable cause" (a reasonable likelihood) to believe that the student had committed a crime, before searching the student. A minor can legally be taken into "protective custody" under circumstances that would not merit a formal legal arrest. But a formal arrest based on "probable cause" is still required before searching a minor.

3. **What If** the officer had found a gun after "frisking" the students even though he hadn't formally arrested them but just took them into custody. Was the frisk legal?

   Answer: Yes. The law distinguishes a "stop and frisk" from an "arrest and search." A police officer may frisk someone who is being questioned if the frisk is for the limited purpose of checking for weapons. This is justified on the grounds that the frisk is only to guarantee the officer's safety and the safety of others. However, if a weapon is found during the frisk, the person who possessed it may be prosecuted if the weapon is possessed illegally.

EXHIBIT "A"

Activities

1. Brainstorm answers to the question: Why did lawmakers of every state pass laws requiring children to attend school until they reach a certain age? The age at which students can drop out of school varies among the states. On the average, states require children to attend school until they are at least sixteen. In some states other factors are taken into account such as employment, completion of a certain grade, family economics, and health reasons. What are the laws in your state regarding age and compulsory education?

2. Role-play a counselor talking to a student who has been offered a job in a gas station. The student (boy or girl) tells you that the owner has promised "big bucks" ($5.00 an hour) and a steady 7-5 job starting next week. What good reasons could you give this person to encourage staying in school? Is a five-dollar-per-hour job really high paying?

3. Bring in the Sunday classified ads from your newspaper. Examine the "Help Wanted" columns. Based on the information you collect in the ads, write a paragraph with a conclusion about skills and education needed to obtain a high-paying job. What is the connection between level of education and income? Why do employers value the educational background of people they want to hire? For how many of the jobs listed in the want ads could you qualify?

4. Organize research teams to find the statistics which indicate the expected annual income or lifetime income for high school dropouts, high school graduates, college graduates, and trained tradespeople. What conclusions can be drawn from this information? Chart these facts for display.

5. **Role Play:** "Congress is now in session." Pretend that the members of the class are Congresspeople. Divide into several "subcommittees." Have each subcommittee write a law which defines the powers of the police to detain juveniles under certain circumstances. Indicate the acceptable reasons for such detention; how long it can last; when parents must be called and under what circumstances the juvenile is to be released into the custody of his or her parents. Indicate at what stage of the process the courts are to be involved.

   After writing the laws, have the committees introduce their proposed legislation to the "Floor" of the Congress. Debate the different versions. Decide on one compromise bill. Have different Congresspeople argue on behalf of parents, teachers, police officers, party store owners, students, principals, video arcade owners and other interested parties. After the debate, vote on the final bill.

Case of the Motorcycle Madness

Motor Vehicle Responsibility

Case of the Motorcycle Madness

Flash Fireball maneuvered his dazzling red Kamikazee Z-200 motorcycle onto the street. He was showing off for all he was worth. He whipped around with abandon and without the protection of a helmet. The law in Flash's state said that Flash had to wear a helmet anytime he rode on his cycle, but Flash said that helmets were definitely, "Un-cool."

> **Flash's motorcycle popped a wheelie for fifty yards down the street.**

Emboldened by a gathering group of admirers, he decided to do his most daring stunt and proceeded to pop wheelies for fifty yards down Woodward Avenue, squealing his tires and drag racing the other cars. To pop a wheelie he had to accelerate so quickly that his front wheel lifted off the ground into the air. He was a virtuoso and only the applause was missing.

At the crescendo of his performance, Grandma Sassy and her baby grandchild were cautiously crossing Woodward Avenue in Grandma's prized 1957 T-Bird, which she was driving to her skydiving lesson. Too late to avoid trouble, Flash's Kamikazee collided with the side of Sassy's T-Bird. Flash and the motorcycle went flying through the air. Grandma and baby screeched to a halt, but not before Grandma Sassy hit the steering wheel and baby hit the dashboard.

The police arrived on the scene where they observed immediately that neither Grandma nor baby were wearing seat belts (which the law required in her state). Flash was laid out flat on the sidewalk and obviously was not wearing a helmet!

What's Your Opinion?

What's Your Opinion?

1. If you were the police officer who saw the whole thing, to whom would you issue traffic tickets (known as citations) and for violations of what laws?

The Law Says:

You would probably issue at least three separate citations to Flash. One ticket for "reckless driving" (based on his popping wheelies and squealing tires), one for failure to wear a helmet, and one for failing to stop in time to avoid the collision (known as "failure to stop in the assured clear distance").

Even though Grandma was not at fault for the accident, the officer should still issue her a ticket for failing to have her seat belt fastened and a second ticket for failing to have her grandchild's seat belt fastened.

What's Your Opinion?

2. Shortly after being released from the hospital, Grandma files a civil lawsuit against Flash in order to make him pay for her wrecked car and hospital bills. In answer to her suit, Flash claims that Grandma was driving too slowly. He also says that since she was not wearing her seat belt, as required by law, Grandma is responsible for her own injuries. Are these arguments valid?

The Law Says:

Yes and No. There is no indication that Grandma was at fault in any way for causing the accident even if she was driving slowly. Therefore, Flash would be responsible for the damage to Grandma's car because his negligence caused the accident. However, the injuries to Grandma and baby are a different story. Because Grandma was violating the law regarding seat belts, she is considered to be "negligent *per se.*" This means that her behavior is defined by law as being negligent. Since the legislature passed the seat belt law to avoid the specific kinds of injury that resulted here, the judge or jury must take Grandma's failure to fasten her seat belt into consideration and reduce the amount of her damage award accordingly.

What's Your Opinion?

3. Are traffic violations civil infractions or criminal infractions?

The Law Says:

Most traffic violations are civil infractions since the guilty motorist only receives a fine. Some serious violations, such as drunk driving, reckless driving, and leaving the scene of an accident without stopping, are criminal misdemeanors, because it is possible to receive a jail sentence on conviction.

What If?

1. **What If** Grandma's state did not have a mandatory seat belt law? Would that make a difference in her lawsuit against Flash Fireball?

   Answer: Yes. If no law actually required seat belt use, Grandma Sassy was under no legal duty to wear it. In that case a judge or jury would not reduce the amount of the award to Grandma.

2. **What If** Flash jumped on his motorcycle immediately after the collision? The police came on the scene and shouted to him to stop, but he raced off in a frenzy without even looking back. Is this a crime? If so, what is the crime?

   Answer: Yes. Flash Fireball is committing several crimes. First, it is unlawful to leave the scene of an accident without identifying yourself. Second, Flash disobeyed the lawful order of a police officer (a crime in most states) and was illegally "fleeing and eluding" the police after the accident.

Activities

1. **You Be the Judge:** Flash decides to contest the citation (ticket) he received for failing to wear a helmet. He has two arguments. First he claims that the helmet law violates his First Amendment right to freely express himself. His second argument is that no one else is affected by his failure to wear a helmet, even if he injures himself.

   The prosecuting attorney for the city argues that there is no constitutional right to ride a motorcycle. Nor is there any symbolic message communicated by riding without a helmet. The prosecutor also notes that there are many costs to society when someone is injured in an auto accident. For example, if Flash has a family, who will support them if Flash cannot work? You be the judge. Write an opinion ruling in favor of or against Flash.

2. Analyze the possible costs to the community if a motorcycle injury seriously disables Flash. (**Answer:** Home care, visiting nurse, ambulance service, hospital insurance, therapy and rehabilitation, unemployment compensation, Social Security benefits for disabled persons, and perhaps financial aid for his family whom he can no longer support.)

3. Conduct a TV street interview with people at the scene to get their reactions to the accident. Let Flash express his views on any laws that would force him to wear a helmet.

4. Does your state require use of motorcycle helmets and/or auto seat belts? If not, write a letter to your state representative stating your views on the issue. If there are laws regulating seat belts and helmets, research how the law has affected traffic injury statistics.

5. Find out from your state department of motor vehicles about the different laws regarding mopeds, motorcycles, and off-road vehicles.

Case of the Super Students

Case of the Super Students

On the first day of school after summer vacation, the parents and students at Bellwether High were invited to a special evening meeting. The results of that meeting shocked and surprised them. The principal, Mr. Knowidall, announced that he had designed an innovative plan for all the Armenian students who, because of their academic superiority, were going to be placed in their own classrooms.

> **"I'm doing this for your own good."**

Knowidall said that Armenians were generally better students because of their ethnic background and cultural values. Though his decision was not based on actual grades or test scores, he was sure his plan would enjoy the approval of the community. As it turned out, the Armenian parents and students were extremely upset. At the next school board meeting they protested that they were victims of discrimination. Mr. Knowidall defended his plan.

"I'm doing this for your own good. This plan will let Armenian students accelerate and at the same time protect regular students from feeling inferior," he said.

The spokesperson for the Armenian families disagreed. "Discrimination based on race or ethnic origin will set these students apart socially and academically from their other classmates," she said. "We believe that segregating students based on race, ethnic background or sex violates the U.S. Constitution and is prohibited by the Civil Rights Acts passed by the Congress of the United States."

Mr. Knowidall argued that although the students would be taught separately, they would all receive equal education.

What's Your Opinion?

What's Your Opinion?

1. Is the principal's plan for separate but equal classes legal or illegal? Explain.

The Law Says:

The plan is illegal. The United States Supreme Court answered this question in the landmark 1954 case of *Brown vs. Board of Education of Topeka.* 347 U.S. 483, 74 S. Ct. 686 (1954). In that case the Court ruled that segregating students by race violates their rights to *equal protection under the law* guaranteed by the Fourteenth Amendment to the *Constitution.* In the *Brown* case, black students in Topeka, Kansas, were denied admission to schools attended by white children until the courts intervened.

What's Your Opinion?

2. Since the *Brown* case was decided, the Congress of the United States has passed a series of civil rights laws that prohibit discrimination based on race, sex, religion or ethnic background. These laws prohibit segregation in all public institutions and all businesses that serve the general public. This means that schools, restaurants, hotels, buses, theaters, airplanes and all other facilities open to the public cannot make people of different races or sexes sit in separate locations or use different facilities. Why do you believe Congress passed this law?

The Law Says:

All people must be treated equally under the law according to the *Constitution.* Segregating people robs them of the right to share all public facilities equally. Congress recognized that when separate facilities were provided for minorities, these facilities were never truly of equal quality.

What's Your Opinion?

3. Can you think of some facilities where it is legal to discriminate on the basis of sex?

The Law Says:

Certain situations are obvious. For example, separate bathrooms for men and women are still allowed. Locker room attendants may be required to be the same sex as those who use the facility. Men and women may have separate sports teams as long as they are provided with equal programs and equal use of facilities. Since the *Constitution* guarantees freedom of religion, religious groups are free to make independent religious decisions. For example, some churches still prohibit women from becoming ordained members of the clergy.

What's Your Opinion?

4. What other kinds of rights do you think are protected by the *Constitution* and the civil rights laws?

The Law Says:

The right to vote, the right to own property, the right to buy a house in any neighborhood or city and the right to equal opportunities for employment are all protected by civil rights laws.

What's Your Opinion?

5. The civil rights laws have been extended to protect rights of the handicapped as well. How does the law assist the handicapped?

The Law Says:

Facilities open to the general public are now required to remove barriers such as steps and narrow doors that block access to handicapped people. Also, employers are prohibited from discriminating against people with handicaps if they are able to do the job.

What If?

1. **What If** all the students in the Bellwether School System were tested for academic performance and, on the basis of the results, students were placed in regular or accelerated classes? After the placement, based on the tests, most of the students of Arabic origin were placed in the accelerated classes. Is the school district guilty of unlawful discrimination in this case?

   Answer: No. In this case the students were separated on the basis of test scores only. Grouping people according to merit is legal as long as the tests are not biased in favor of one group over another. However, any testing or any program which seemed to favor one group and/or exclude another would undergo very close examination to be sure that the selection procedure gives everyone an equal chance.

2. **What If** a man and a woman score equally high on an employment test? The employer currently employs fifty men and two women. Is it legal, in this case, to favor the woman applicant over the man if it is proven that in the past the employer refused to hire women, based on their sex?

   Answer: Yes. In cases where an employer's past employment practices have created a serious imbalance based on race or sex, then it is proper to take race or sex into account to remedy past unfairness. If both candidates are qualified for the job, the employer can choose the one to hire or promote based on sex or race, to correct past discrimination. This is known in the law as *affirmative action*.

Activities

1. Only men are *drafted* to serve in the armed forces during times of war. The Supreme Court upheld the constitutionality of this policy. How do you feel about the fairness of having only men being forced to fight in times of war?

   Divide the class randomly into two groups PRO and CON. Each group will stand at opposite ends of the room. All class members may participate by presenting arguments to support their respective group position, PRO or CON, re: Should women be drafted and should women serve in combat? The point of this strategy is to be persuasive and convince members of the opposing side to come over and join your ranks. Those who have changed sides may be given an opportunity to explain what convinced them to change their minds.

2. In World War II when the U.S. was at war with Japan, Germany and Italy, Japanese-Americans were singled out as a threat to national security. In 1942, 112,000 Japanese-Americans living on the west coast were forced to leave everything, sell their businesses and homes, and were then sent to detention camps for the duration of the war. Of this number, 70,000 were American citizens, many of whom were born in the U.S.A. There was never any evidence that these people were in any way disloyal to this country. Interestingly, German-Americans and Italian-Americans were not treated in this shocking way. One supposed justification for discriminating against Japanese-Americans was the fear created by the surprise Japanese attack on Pearl Harbor.

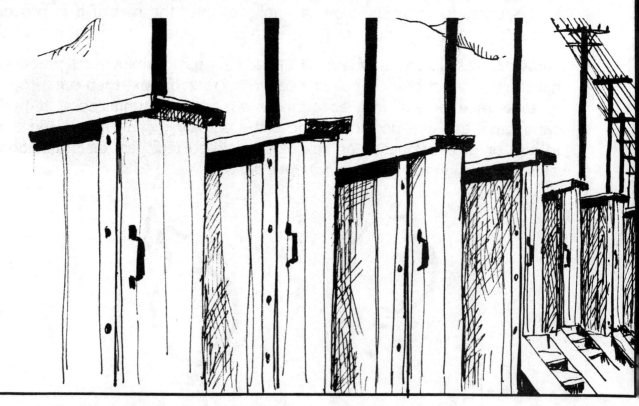

Write a letter to your best friend. Pretend you are a U.S. citizen of Japanese descent living in San Francisco in 1943. Even though you were born in the United States, have never been to Japan, and are a loyal U.S. citizen, you and your family are about to be sent to a detention camp in Wyoming. Your parents are forced to sell their business for less than it is worth. Your older brother is in the U.S. Army fighting for the United States and at the same time the rest of your family is being deprived of their rights. Today is your last day of school in San Francisco before being sent away. What would you say in your letter to your non-Japanese friend so that he/she will understand how you feel? You are being taken away from your home and everything you have ever known for an indefinite time, as if you were a criminal. How would this disrupt your life? Why is it unfair?

3. In 1987 there was a bill in Congress proposing that our government pay 1.3 billion dollars to the surviving victims of the Japanese-American incarceration to compensate them for this miscarriage of justice against an entire group of people in America. Did this bill pass? Write to your Congressperson to find out.

4. On occasion, legislatures pass laws which are later ruled to be unconstitutional. The process of overturning those laws is often a long and arduous one. A perfect example of how unconstitutional laws can be changed lies in the history of the U.S. civil rights movement.

In one such case, a law in Montgomery, Alabama, required black people to ride in the rear of public buses. One day, in 1954, a hard-working black woman, Rosa Parks, after a long day of work, refused to give up her seat in the front of the bus to a white man. She felt that the law was wrong and decided to assert her rights. Her arrest led ultimately to that law being declared unconstitutional.

She was supported by the Reverend Martin Luther King, Jr., who led a boycott of the Montgomery bus system. Boycotts were also illegal under Alabama law. The civil rights workers at all times remained peaceful and nonviolent, even when violence was used against them. Ultimately, their courageous efforts were rewarded as old, unconstitutional laws were struck down by courts, and new laws were passed to guard the civil rights of minorities and all Americans. Unless these people had stood up for their rights, those unjust laws might never have changed.

With regard to the case of the Japanese-American internment during World War II and the laws which enforced segregation of black people in this country, discuss the following:

- Is the price of freedom eternal vigilance?
- Are laws a reflection of the society that makes them?
- Are laws only as just as the people who enforce them?
- Are those who sit idly by and allow injustice to occur as much to blame for society's injustices as those who actually commit them?
- When one person is robbed of his or her legal rights, how does this threaten everyone's rights?
- How can such injustice be avoided in the future?

For the Teacher

In 1943 Japanese-Americans took their case to the U.S. Supreme Court. They argued that they were being singled out based solely on their race, which violated their constitutional right to Equal Protection of the law.

Unfortunately, wartime hysteria prevailed. In 1944 the Supreme Court ruled against those U.S. citizens in the cases of *Hirabayashi vs. United States** and *Korematsu vs. United States*.** Today those decisions are widely criticized by modern legal scholars. The majority of the court wrote that although

". . . nothing short of apprehension by the proper military authorities of the gravest imminent danger to the public safety can constitutionally justify [those laws] . . . exclusion of those of Japanese origin was deemed necessary because of the presence of an unascertained number of disloyal members of the group, most of whom we have no doubt were loyal to this country."

Not all members of the court agreed. Three of the nine justices *dissented.* This means that they opposed the decision of the majority and wrote dissenting opinions. The dissenters wrote that the relocation law

". . . goes over the very brink of constitutional power and falls into the ugly abyss of racism . . . . To be valid, . . . it is necessary only that the action have some reasonable relation to the removal of the dangers of invasion, sabotage or espionage. But the exclusion . . . of all persons with Japanese blood in their veins has no such reasonable relation . . . . There was no adequate proof . . . . Not one person of Japanese ancestry was accused or convicted of espionage or sabotage after Pearl Harbor while they were still free, a fact which is some evidence of the loyalty of the vast majority of these individuals . . . . It seems incredible that . . . it would have been impossible to hold loyalty hearings for the [individuals] involved—especially when a large part of their number represented children and elderly men and women. Any inconvenience [to the government] that may have accompanied an attempt to conform to procedural due process***, cannot be said to justify violations of constitutional rights of individuals.

"I dissent, because I think the indisputable facts exhibit a clear violation of constitutional rights."

*Hirabayashi vs. U.S 320 U.S. 81 (1944)
**Korematsu vs. U.S. 323 U.S. 214 (1944)
***by holding loyalty hearings.

Case of the Math Menace

Case of the Math Menace

Maggie Metric was the very best math student in the class at Einstein High. Competitive excitement was running strong because of the announcement of a scholarship prize to be awarded to the math student with the highest cumulative grade for the year. Lester Loutish was the strong second place student and was doing everything he could to beat Maggie for first place. The trouble was, he was not always the most ethical person in the world. Just before a big test, Lester got a brainstorm.

Maggie Metric is a cheater!

As his competitor, Maggie, passed his desk, he whispered to her, "I hear you're so good because you steal test answers from the teacher."

Flushed and angry, Maggie took her seat. She prepared for the test, quite shaken by the awful lie! Encouraged with this bold strategy, Lester tried again on the day of the next big test. Before math class, he sneaked into the empty room and wrote in huge letters on the board, "Maggie Metric is a math cheat!"

In minutes the entire class filed in and read the false message. When Maggie came in she broke into tears. The shocked teacher entered and briskly erased the board. Maggie was so rattled by the episode that she scored poorly on that day's exam. Because of her weak performance on that critical exam, she did not win the scholarship.

What's Your Opinion?

What's Your Opinion?

1. What civil law has Lester Loutish broken?

The Law Says:

Lester has committed two "torts" against Maggie. (*Tort* is the French word for "wrong.") One tort he committed is called "intentional infliction of emotional distress." He is also guilty of "defamation of character," also known as "libel." (Verbally communicated defamation of character is called slander. Written defamation of character is called libel.) Defaming someone is defined as "making a statement about another person that is materially false or misleading and which tends to damage the victim's reputation."

What's Your Opinion?

2. Has Lester Loutish committed a crime against Maggie Metric?

The Law Says:

No. Although he has violated civil law, his offense is not considered to be a criminal act.

What If?

1. **What If** Lester Loutish made his false accusations directly to Maggie Metric's face, but no one else heard? Is this slander? Why?

   Answer: No, it is not slander. To be slanderous or libelous, the false statements must injure one's reputation. To injure a reputation, the statements must be communicated to a third party (either heard or read).

2. **What If** Maggie proves that Lester's lies so upset her that she blew the exam and lost the scholarship and that his lies gave her a bad reputation? What remedies could a court award her?

Answer: A court could order Lester to pay Maggie an amount of money equal to her lost scholarship. A court could also order Lester to pay Maggie money to compensate her for the damage to her reputation and an appropriate amount of money for the emotional harm done to Maggie. A court could also issue an *injunction* against Lester ordering him to "cease and desist" (stop and discontinue) his harassment of Maggie. If Lester violated the "cease and desist" order he could be fined or even jailed.

3. **What If** Lester Loutish heard a rumor that the Mayor of Anytown had taken a bribe? Lester tells all his friends before he finds out that the rumor is false, and he stops circulating the lie. Can the Mayor successfully sue Lester for defamation of character?

   Answer: No. Public figures, such as politicians, receive less protection from libel and slander than people who are not in the public spotlight. To win a defamation suit, public figures must prove not only that the statements are false, but also that the person who made them acted with *malice*. Malice means that the person making the statements knew they were false and tried to intentionally injure the reputation of the public figure.

Activities

1. **Discussion:** Why do you think it is a good idea to make it more difficult for public officials to successfully sue for defamation of character? (**Answer:** The U.S. Supreme Court answered this question in the case of *New York Times vs. Sullivan* 376 U.S. 255; 84 S. Ct. 710 [1964].)

In setting the "actual malice" standard, the court noted two things: First, public officials themselves are granted immunity from libel lawsuits for false remarks they make (if made in the course of their official duties) unless made with "actual malice." Otherwise, the court reasoned, "the threat of lawsuits would inhibit the fearless, vigorous and effective administration of government."* Therefore, the court felt if public officials are immune from libel suits, so should those people be who criticize them in good faith.

The second point noted by the court was that if public officials could sue people for innocently made, though false, statements, then,

> "would-be critics of official conduct may be deterred from voicing their criticism, even though it is believed to be true, and even though it is, in fact, true, because of doubt whether it can be proved in court or fear of the expense of having to prove it in court."*

New York Times vs. Sullivan, Supra.

91

If public officials could successfully sue people for making false statements made in good faith, the court felt it would "dampen the vigor and limit the variety of public debate. It would be inconsistent with the First and Fourteenth Amendments."*

2. **Two-Way Role Play:** Assign one student to play President Ronald Reagan. Assign another student to play the editor of the *New York Times*. President Reagan is furious because the *Times* just printed a story accusing him of masterminding the plot to sell weapons to Iran and then using the profits to illegally support the Contra Rebels in Nicaragua. Mr. Reagan wants the paper to print a retraction. The editor does not want to back down. He thinks the story is true, but it is hard to prove.

Play the scene twice. First, play it knowing the libel law as set forth in *New York Times vs. Sullivan*. Then play it as if the court had ruled that public officials could sue newspapers and win defamation suits more easily. **Hint:** If the *Sullivan* decision had allowed defamation suits by public officials, the official would threaten the editor with lawsuits that would put his newspaper out of business. Thanks to *Sullivan,* as decided, however, the public official is limited to less coercive types of persuasion when dealing with the editor.

Note to the Teacher: You may choose to replace President Reagan with a more current political figure in controversy or a different person in history or literature.

3. From your standpoint as a person knowledgeable in the law of defamation, what would you explain to someone who quoted the nursery rhyme, "Sticks and stones will break my bones, but names can never hurt me"?

4. There is a frequently repeated quote that goes, "I don't care what you print about me as long as you spell my name right!" If you were to guess at the kind of person who would make such a remark, who do you think it might be? Explain the reasons for your answer.

5. Look up the word *reputation* in the dictionary. Why does the law protect a person's reputation?

Can you think of a situation where a famous person's reputation was damaged? How could such damage affect one's future?

"THEY SAY HE CHOPPED DOWN HIS FATHER'S CHERRY TREE YEARS AGO."

Case of the Neighborly Nuisance

Nuisance

Case of the Neighborly Nuisance

One warm summer night, Boris Boomer decided to have a party. He called all of his friends and by 11:00 that night everybody was having a blast. Everyone but Boris's neighbors, that is. Boris's thousand-watt stereo and his boisterous buddies frolicking on the front lawn were disturbing people all over the block. Not only that, but the smoke from Boris's barbecue was wafting right into the open window of his neighbor, Fester Fusebox. Finally, Mr. Fusebox blew up. He called Boris on the phone.

> **The smoke wafted into Mr. Fusebox's open window.**

"Enough is enough, Boomer," said Mr. Fusebox, fuming. "Your friends are acting like an invading army, your stereo is keeping people awake for miles around and the smoke belching from your barbecue is choking my whole family. Send your guests home or I'll call the police!"

"Hey man, it's a free country," responded Boris. "I can do what I want on my own property. If you don't like it, close your windows."

The frustrated Fusebox finally called the police.

What's Your Opinion?

What's Your Opinion?
1. Whose rights will prevail here? Boris's right to party or Mr. Fusebox's right to reasonable peace and quiet?

The Law Says:
Mr. Fusebox has the right to peaceful enjoyment of his property—especially late at night.

What's Your Opinion?
2. Boris's behavior is known legally as a *nuisance*. Can you think of a definition of nuisances and list some?

The Law Says:
A nuisance is any activity that disturbs or interferes with other people's rights to enjoy and use their own property. Loud parties, barking dogs, burning leaves and barbecues, smelly garbage piles, constantly noisy equipment, late night disturbances, littering, and even letting weeds and grass grow too long, all can be nuisances.

What's Your Opinion?
3. What can Mr. Fusebox do to get Boris to be quiet?

The Law Says:
If Mr. Fusebox calls the police, they will probably issue Boris a ticket or violation notice if the noise is still loud when the police arrive. Most cities have ordinances prohibiting loud noisemaking between certain hours and regulating activities that may become nuisances. Violating these ordinances may be civil infractions or misdemeanors.

What If?

1. **What If** right after receiving the complaint from the neighbors, Boris turns off his stereo, moves his barbecue so it doesn't bother Mr. Fusebox and makes his guests quiet down? Would Boris still receive a ticket?

   Answer: Probably not. If Boris promptly "abates" or eliminates the nuisance after being notified he is disturbing his neighbors, there is nothing more to complain about.

2. **What If** a nuisance continues for a long period of time even after a complaint? What can the neighbors do?

   Answer: The neighbors could go to court and file a lawsuit against the offender. If the neighbors succeed, the court would issue a court order, known as an injunction, ordering a halt to the nuisance. Violating or ignoring the injunction could result in fines or even jail time for the offender.

Activities

1. Farmer Fred owned a farm since 1969 where he grew crops and raised pigs, sheep, and cows far from the city. By 1987, the city grew toward the farm and some developers bought the farm next door. They built houses in the meadow, put the babbling brook into a sewer, and then named the subdivision Meadow Brook Farms.

   After the homes were bought and families moved in, they complained that Farmer Fred was creating a nuisance. He often plowed his fields with a noisy tractor early in the morning. Even worse, his animals smelled and he sprayed chemicals on his crops which was carried by the wind to the new houses.

   Discuss the concept of "coming to the nuisance" as illustrated by this story and why it might make a difference. Think about how we must balance the rights of property owners who have different interests from each other. Why does society have an interest in preserving farms even though it may not be easy to live next to them? How can laws help in such situations?

   Role-play a town meeting at which these issues are discussed. A chairperson calls the meeting to order with the following participants: Fred and other farmers, customers who eat Fred's crops, protesting land developers, workers, home owners and county officials.

2. Concerning the limits to freedom there is an expression in the law that says: "One person's rights extend only as far as the other guy's nose." Write an essay on what this means.

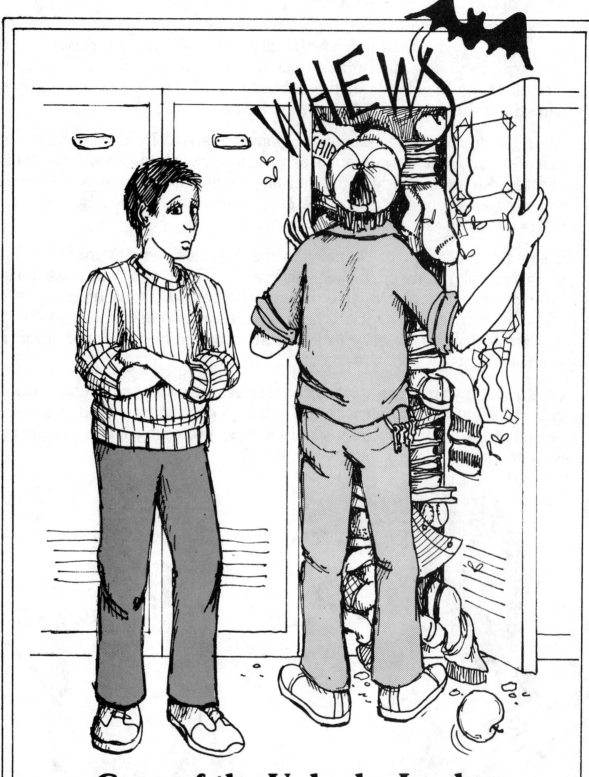

Case of the Unlucky Locker

Case of the Unlucky Locker

One dismal Monday morning, a rumor ran through Anytown Middle School that someone had brought a handgun to school and was showing off. By lunchtime the rumor spread around the community as well. Concerned parents were calling the school to determine what was being done to apprehend the culprit and protect the students. Over the loudspeaker came the announcement that all lockers were to be opened by the custodian before dismissal

> **Incredibly dirty laundry was rotting in his locker.**

time. Kenny Compost, a seventh grader, had some incredibly dirty laundry rotting in his locker. When the search arrived at his locker, he was so embarrassed that he refused to open the combination lock. The custodian was told to bring out the bolt cutter and, over Kenny's protests, began to cut through the lock.

What's Your Opinion?

What's Your Opinion?

1. Read the Fourth Amendment to the Constitution. Does the school have the right to search students' lockers without a warrant? Explain.

The Law Says:

Yes. The logic is that the lockers actually belong to the school and not to the individual students who use them. Another reason: The school has a responsibility to protect its students. It has also been held that the Fourth Amendment applies only to police—not to school officials. Some courts have stated that school officials are *in loco parentis*. Therefore, they have the right to search the students' lockers just as parents do.

What's Your Opinion?

2. Privacy is known as a "fundamental right." The most important civil rights, granted or implied by the Constitution are all known in the law as *fundamental rights*. List the rights you believe are fundamental and why.

The Law Says:

The fundamental rights are freedom of speech, press, assembly, and religion. Freedom to travel without restriction, the right to privacy, the right to marry and have children, the right to due process and equal protection under law, and the right to vote.

What's Your Opinion?

3. The Supreme Court has decided that the government can only interfere with fundamental rights where there is a "compelling state interest." That means there must be an extremely important reason. What compelling reasons would justify regulations limiting freedom of speech? Freedom of religion? Freedom to marry?

The Law Says:

(a) Freedom of speech has been limited in cases where the speech incited people to violence or involved a plan to overthrow the government by force or violence. (b) Polygamy is illegal even though some religions permit it. (c) Freedom to marry each other is not granted to brothers and sisters in order to avoid genetic inbreeding.

What If?

1. **What If** the police arrived on the scene and proceeded to search all of the lockers without a warrant? Would they have the legal right to do that?

   Answer: No. The Fourth Amendment prohibits searches by police agencies unless they have a warrant signed by a judge.

2. **What If** just as they enter the school, students are required to pass through metal detectors? Those students found with weapons are suspended or expelled from school after a hearing. Is this legal?

   Answer: So far, yes. This practice is used in several cities in the United States where guns in schools have created serious problems. Although some people criticize the practice as being an improper infringement of students' rights of privacy, the courts have not forbidden the practice. The U.S. Supreme Court has not ruled on the issue as of late 1987. (Research the status of such practices in your state.)

3. **What If**, as a result of the locker search, the principal finds controlled substances (drugs, weapons) or other contraband in someone's locker? What could the principal do?

   Answer: The principal could (a) hold a hearing which could result in disciplinary action including expulsion, (b) call in the parents, and/or (c) turn the material over to the police.

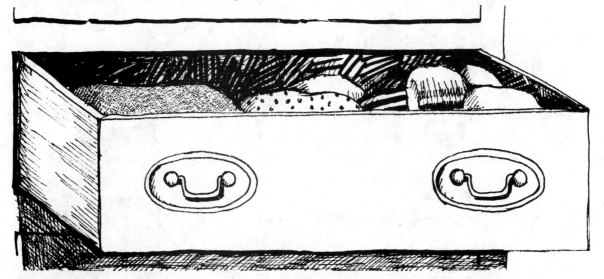

4. **What If** your father discovered something illegal in your dresser drawer and turned it over to the police? Is this legal? Can the police use the evidence against you in court?

   Answer: Yes. It is a legal search and the evidence is admissible in court. The "exclusionary rule" (see Glossary) applies only to searches conducted by the police and people working for the police.

Activities

1. **Write** a paragraph in answer to the following question: Why is it necessary for the police to have a warrant to search your home, yet no warrant or probable cause is necessary to search your luggage before boarding a plane?

   Answer: The privacy of one's own home is considered so sacred that the police may enter only with a search warrant, authorized by a judge. The airport, however, is a place where people do not expect the same amount of privacy. This is a case where individual rights must bend to the overriding need to guarantee the safety of all passengers. Also, airline personnel are not police and so are not required to obtain a search warrant to search those entering the airlines' private property.

2. **Debate** the following proposition:
   Terrorism is such a serious problem that the police should be allowed to search any home or any person at any time, without a warrant, to combat the threat.

3. **Discuss** and/or write your views on these questions:
   a. Is it important to limit the power of the police? Why or why not?
   b. Can the police be limited in their power and still effectively fight crime and enforce the law?
   c. What would be the result of unlimited power by the police?
   d. What would result if there were no police force?
   e. How do we balance the individual's rights to privacy and the need of society to maintain order and enforce the law?

4. **Invite** a police officer to your class to discuss the above issues. Also contact the local branch of the American Civil Liberties Union and invite one of their members to discuss the same topics with your class.

5. Read and discuss George Orwell's novel, *1984.* Is this chilling tale a realistic portrayal of the ultimate government invasion of privacy and the rights of the individual? How does this loss of freedom occur?

6. Where do we draw the line when we say, "the good of the group outweighs the rights of the individual"? This position seems very sensible in the context of airport safety. But people concerned about "civil liberties" regard this as a dangerous first step toward a loss of other freedoms. Can you think of an example illustrating the dangers of the will of the majority destroying the rights of the individual?

Case of the Suspended Student

Case of the Suspended Student

Stanley Steadfast was walking to school one fine fall morning. His neighbor, Peter Pyro, was burning a gigantic pile of fallen leaves. The smoke billowed from the fire and polluted the entire neighborhood. Stanley couldn't escape the smoke which clung to his clothing.

> **"Don't I get a chance to explain?"**

When Stanley walked into the school, he passed by the assistant principal, Mr. Stickler, who smelled the smoke immediately.

Hey there, Steadfast," bellowed Mr. Stickler. "You've been smoking marijuana, haven't you?"

"No, sir. It was just leaves that . . ."

"Don't get smart with me, young man. Go to the office."

The obedient Steadfast walked to the office—despite his innocence. Soon after, Mr. Stickler entered the office and announced, "Steadfast, you know that smoking marijuana is a crime. I'm expelling you."

"Don't I get a chance to explain?" pleaded Stanley.

"There's nothing to explain. I'm sorry, but rules are rules. I've got no choice."

What's Your Opinion?

What's Your Opinion?

1. Was Mr. Stickler's behavior appropriate?

The Law Says:

No. Expulsion is a very serious punishment. Before a student can be subjected to such discipline, he or she has the right to a fair and complete hearing. That is to say, the student has the right to expect *due process of law*.

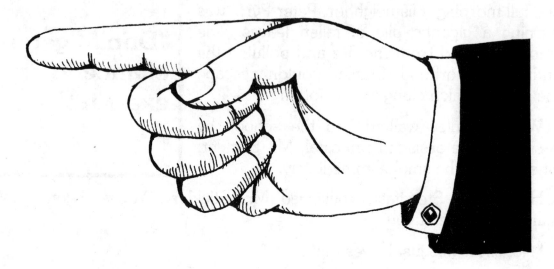

What's Your Opinion?

2. What should such a process consist of?

The Law Says:

The United States Supreme Court has ruled that if the suspension is for ten days or less, the student must be informed, orally or in writing, the exact charges being made against him and the evidence the authorities have. The student must also have the opportunity to present his side of the story.*

For suspensions of over ten days, or for total expulsion from school, a more formal procedure may be required.** Such process could include a hearing in front of an impartial fact finder, and perhaps allow the student to be represented by an attorney at the hearing. The exact process will vary from state to state.

The court has ruled that education is a legal right that cannot be taken away without due process of law.

Goss vs. Lopez, 419 U.S. 565, 95 S. Ct. 729, 42 L.Ed2d. 725 (1975).

**Ibid.

What If?

1. **What If** Stanley Steadfast was expelled after a hearing but still wanted to prove his innocence? What could he do?

   Answer: Eventually Stanley might have to file a lawsuit in court. Before he can do that, however, he must first go through all of the normal channels and appeals with the school's administration. (This is known as "exhausting the administrative remedies.") He should appeal his case in writing to higher school officials, such as the principal and the school board. It would probably be worthwhile for Stanley and his parents to hire an attorney as early in the process as possible.

   If Stanley is unsuccessful with the school officials, then he might consider filing a lawsuit. Although this might be a costly and time-consuming process, the issues are serious enough and Stanley's case is strong enough that it might be worth the fight.

2. **What If** Mr. Stickler actually saw Tommy Toker smoking marijuana in the parking lot and confiscated a bag of alleged marijuana from him? Could Tommy be expelled without a hearing in that case?

   Answer: No. Even in a clear case, the student is still entitled to a hearing (due process).

3. **What If** Sally Sharpshooter is firing paper wads at the back of Billy Bumpkin's head? Mr. Niceguy, the teacher, has been warning Sally all period to cut it out. Finally, in exasperation, Mr. Niceguy says, "OK, that's it! Go to the principal's office right now for your disruptive behavior."

"I don't have to," says Sally, sharply. "I demand due process—a jury trial, an attorney."

What are Sally's chances of avoiding an immediate trip to the office.

Answer: Slim and none. Although Sally would be entitled to "due process" if threatened with suspension or expulsion, the teacher has the right to keep order in the class. Students have the responsibility to respect the rights of others. If the teacher attempts to remove the student for long periods of time, then the punishment begins to resemble a suspension which would require a hearing of some sort with other school officials.

With further regard to discipline—some states allow teachers to use "corporal punishment," such as spanking students, in order to maintain discipline. Some states, however, forbid corporal punishment.

Activities

1. Hold a debate. One side will take the position that to maintain discipline in the schools, the principal and the teachers should be free to expel and suspend students at will. The other side will argue that in school, as in society, a student is innocent until proven guilty and to short cut due process is as unacceptable in school as it is everywhere else.

2. Stanley Steadfast's parents are convinced that their son is innocent. His dad believes that an innocent person does not need a lawyer to represent him. His mother believes that he does need a lawyer. Put yourself in the place of either parent and write a page explaining your position. Who do you think is right? Read your position papers in class.

   Argument for the dad's position that a lawyer is unnecessary: He would like to believe that the truth will come through and that it should not be necessary to call in an outsider. He might also argue that when you hire an attorney it appears as if you are guilty and that's why you need a lawyer. (Some people believe that an attorney will unnecessarily inflame the situation.)

   Argument for the mom's position that a lawyer is necessary: By hiring a lawyer, the other side will know that you are very serious about defending your rights. A lawyer also knows the important details of the law that can help make your case more forceful. It helps to have someone be your advocate and speak for you who is not so emotionally involved with the situation.

3. With a small committee, make an appointment to talk with your principal or assistant principal about school policy concerning discipline and suspensions. Like intelligent interviewers, prepare your questions in advance. The entire class should discuss and select the questions of most concern to everyone. Make a report to the class of the principal's answers. Perhaps the committee could get permission to use a tape recorder during the interview.

4. What if Stanley Steadfast asked you to defend him against the assistant principal, Mr. Stickler? What are some of the arguments you would use to convince a committee of your friend's innocence? Why is the case against Stanley a weak one?

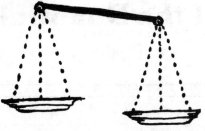

Case of the Doubtful Dopers

Substance Abuse

Case of the Doubtful Dopers

After the school dance, a rumor spread that someone made arrangements for a party to wrap up the evening. It turned out to be true. Sid Smarm, one of the students, rented a room at the Sleazy Rest Motel and invited the most popular kids. He did loosen up a bit and included some of the less important people who were really flattered to have been invited. Everybody was in good spirits when out of the blue, someone started smoking marijuana. The joints were being passed around and the laughter and mood was contagious. Most of the kids weren't smoking and were looking pretty uncomfortable, but nonetheless, they didn't leave. Nobody wanted to walk out on a party of the elite and make themselves look like wimps.

Sid rented a room at the Sleazy Rest Motel.

The odor of the marijuana soon wafted through the motel hallways, and the owner was alerted by a very concerned guest. The owner called the police who arrived promptly on the scene and arrested everyone in the room. Several of the students protested vigorously that they were absolutely not smoking the stuff at all. The police continued to round up everybody in the room and said unsympathetically, "Tell it to the judge!"

What's Your Opinion?

What's Your Opinion?
1. What crimes were committed by the students?

The Law Says:
Those who were actually smoking the marijuana were guilty of "possession or use of a controlled substance."

What's Your Opinion?
2. Were the students who were not smoking guilty of a crime?

The Law Says:
Even those students who were not smoking pot, but who knew that marijuana was being used, could be guilty of "frequenting an establishment where illegal activity occurred" (a misdemeanor).

What If?

1. **What If** the case of all the students came to trial and the nonsmokers were also accused of marijuana possession? Can the nonsmokers be convicted?

    Answer: Yes. Even the nonsmokers can be convicted if the judge or jury does not believe that they were indeed just hanging around and watching the smokers!

2. **What If** you innocently find yourself in a place where there are drugs, or firearms or stolen merchandise? How can you protect yourself?

    Answer: The practical answer here is that the only way to avoid such legal entanglements is to immediately leave the premises at the first sign of illegal behavior?

Activities

1. How would you explain to someone in your class, who was really naive, all the things that could happen to a person from using illegal drugs? (**Answer:** A person could be fined, suspended from school, have a serious blemish on school records, be jailed, or become addicted. Even if you are not caught, drugs can affect your grades, personality, and emotional and physical health.)

2. Role-play a situation where a student in your school is really trying hard to convince you to buy or try an illegal substance. How would you discourage him? What would be the best way to deal with the situation? What arguments would the pusher use?

Case of the Cartoon Copycat

Copyright/Plagiarism

Case of the Cartoon Copycat

Pedro Picasso was the best artist in the whole school. Everyone admired his great drawings. His favorite subjects were other students and teachers whom he would capture in various funny poses. One day the governor of the state came to speak to an assembly in Pedro's high school. Pedro drew a pencil sketch of the governor as he spoke to the students. It was a very good likeness in Pedro's usual humorous style. He drew the governor's ears slightly larger than they actually were and his bushy hair wilder than real life. Everybody loved it. To make sure he got credit for his drawing and to make sure no one could copy it without his permission, Pedro signed his drawing at the bottom with the following notice, "Copyright 1987 Pedro Picasso." Then he tacked a copy of the sketch on the school bulletin board.

> **"Picasso was the best artist in the whole school."**

The next day, Manny Moneymaker made a copy of Pedro's drawing on a copy machine and sold it to a local newspaper, complete with Pedro's copyright notice at the bottom.

What's Your Opinion?

What's Your Opinion?

1. Copyrights are the legal rights granted by Congress to artists, authors, music composers and creators of *original* works. Copyrights give the creators and their agents the exclusive right to use, sell or copy their work for their lifetime, plus fifty years. Why do you think Congress created copyrights?

The Law Says:

If creative people could not control the fruits of their labor, their incentive to create would be reduced. Hence, Congress wrote the copyright law to protect what is known as "intellectual property."

What's Your Opinion?

2. Did Manny Moneymaker violate the copyright law?

The Law Says:

Yes. Manny committed "copyright infringement." This means that Manny used Pedro's property illegally by reproducing and selling it without Pedro's permission.

What's Your Opinion?

3. Why was it necessary for Pedro to put his copyright notice on his drawing to preserve his copyright?

The Law Says:

Notice is a very important part of the law. The copyright notice tells the world that Pedro intends to assert his rights. The notice must be placed where it can be clearly seen, otherwise the copyright is not good. If Pedro, or any artist or author, publishes his work without putting the notice on it, the work becomes "public domain." Anyone is free to use public domain works.

What's Your Opinion?

4. What remedies can Pedro seek from Manny Moneymaker for illegally using Pedro's cartoon?

The Law Says:

If Pedro had filed his copyright with the Register of Copyrights in Washington, D.C., he could file a lawsuit against Manny. Pedro would be entitled to any money Manny received. Pedro could also obtain an injunction (a court order) prohibiting Manny from using Pedro's drawing. Under some circumstances, Manny would also receive a fine.

What's Your Opinion?

5. What is *plagiarism*?

The Law Says:

Plagiarism is a form of cheating. It is defined as "claiming someone else's work as your own." Copying from a book without giving the author credit is plagiarism. So is copying someone else's homework or test answer.

What's Your Opinion?

6. Is plagiarism a violation of the law?

The Law Says:

Yes. Plagiarism is a form of *fraud*. Fraud is defined as "obtaining something of value unlawfully by deception or trick." When a student plagiarizes, he/she is trying to fraudulently obtain a grade or a diploma or a college degree. Plagiarism is also a violation of the copyright law if the plagiarized work has a copyright.

Plagiarism is a violation of school rules because it violates educational ethics of honest scholarship.

What's Your Opinion?

7. What penalities may teachers or school officials impose for plagiarism?

The Law Says:

Teachers and school administrators are free to administer whatever punishments they feel are proper, depending on the seriousness of each case. They are limited in three ways: (a) They must treat all students the same for similar infractions. (b) There should be a fair *process* to avoid punishing an innocent person. (c) The punishment should not be excessive.

Punishments can vary from lowering a grade on a single paper or test all the way to expulsion from school in extremely serious cases in colleges or universities.

What's Your Opinion?

8. What is the difference between a copyright, a patent, and a trademark?

The Law Says:

Copyrights give creators of original artistic, literary and musical works the exclusive control over their works for the lifetime of the author plus fifty years. Patents are granted to inventors of new and useful inventions. Patents give inventors exclusive control of their inventions for seventeen years. Trademarks are the symbols, logos, labels, and brand names that identify and distinguish one product from another. Trademarked goods are marked with the symbol TM or ® (meaning registered). Trademarks are good as long as the product is sold in commerce. Patents, trademarks, and copyrights all fall under the category of "intellectual property" and are granted by the U.S. government in Washington, D.C.

What If?

1. **What If** you are doing a research paper on American poets? In the course of your research you want to copy poems from different books, but you see that there is a copyright notice in each of the books and a statement which prohibits copying. Can you legally make copies or include those poems in your paper?

   Answer: Yes. The copyright law makes a specific exception for scholarly and educational copying which is not done for profit. This is known as "Fair Use." However, it is always required by custom to *give full credit* to any author or poet whose work you copy.

2. **What If** you have written a rock and roll song that you want to send off to your favorite group or to a music publisher? How can you protect yourself and avoid a rip-off?

   Answer: This is one case where filing a formal copyright application with the Register of Copyrights in Washington, D.C., would make sense to protect your work. Also, it is extremely important to place the copyright notice on your work before showing it to anyone. The reason for filing a formal copyright application is to prove the exact date you published your work. Another way to prove the date of your publication is to have the original song notarized and dated by a Notary Public. (**Warning:** People often think they can prove the date of their creations by mailing a copy of their work to themselves. Most courts do not accept the mail technique as a valid date marker.)

Activities

1. Assert your legal rights! Produce a short story, a poem, a song, a cartoon, a blueprint, an original dessert recipe or a picture of your very own clown face. (Yes! Clown faces are copyrightable.)

   In order to be valid, a copyright notice must use the word *copyright* or use the letter *c* in a circle (©) followed by the year of the first publication and the name of the holder of the copyright. (The holder who is the owner of the copyright may be the author or someone to whom the author has sold the rights, such as the publisher.) All information must be legible to be legal. Look inside a book on the title page to see how this information is recorded. If you want more protection, you may want to file your copyright with the government. For information, write to the Copyright Office, Library of Congress, Washington, D.C. 20540.

2. Turn to the comics in your daily newspaper. Look carefully at a cartoon of your choice. Somewhere in the frames you will see information written in small print. Record what you see (the artist's name, the date and month of the paper in which the comic appeared, the name of the syndicate and the year in which the strip was copyrighted "© 1989, United Feature Syndicate" or "©1989, King Feature Syndicate, Inc., World Rights reserved"). How does all this protect the artist's work?

3. Role-play some scenes from the following situation: Valerie Volley is the school tennis champ. The athlete is doing poorly in one of her classes, though she's really working her head off. On Monday night, Valerie calls her friend Wally Goodheart because she is desperately in need of help. "I've got this paper due on 'Honesty,' and it's just about killing me," she tells Wally. "I keep writing it over and over but it's still as clear as mud! You've gotta help me."

   Some Scenario Possibilities for Role Play:
   - Wally Goodheart gives Valerie Volley his own paper from last semester and is found out by his own teacher who is disappointed. Wally tries to defend his action.
   - Valerie discovers a book that is perfect and copies a chapter word for word. When the teacher discovers what Val has done, she calls Val in to speak with her. Val doesn't understand what the fuss is all about.
   - A counselor has a talk with both Wally Goodheart and Valerie Volley. They talk about ethics and moral character.
   - The teacher flunks Valerie causing her to become ineligible for the tennis team. Tennis fans in the community blame the teacher for making unreasonable demands on Valerie. At a parent-teacher meeting, Val's fans vent all their anger about the teacher's treatment of their prize-winning athlete.

4. A group of students are preparing speeches and dramatic interpretations for a school contest. The best presenter is using a speech from an old book she found and is pretending that it is her own original work. Only you recognize the speech as the work of another author. Despite the hard work of all the other students, this girl is going to win easily because the speech is so funny and professional. What is your responsibility in the matter? What would you do?

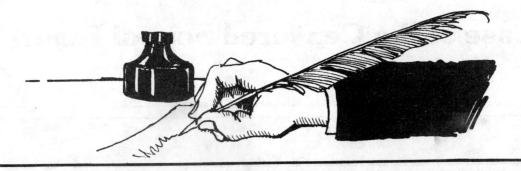

119

Case of the Censored School Paper

Case of the Censored School Paper

This exercise is the culmination of your study of the law and your legal research skills. Now that you are familiar with much legal terminology, theory and practice, it is time to take your newly acquired skill out of the world of legal theory and into the world of real courtroom decisions. In October 1987, a very important case came up from St. Louis, Missouri, which obviously belongs in *Everyday Law for Young Citizens*.

Are student newspapers protected by the First Amendment?

The case of the *Hazelwood School District vs. Cathy Kuhlmeier* (noted in the *Detroit Free Press* article) has just been argued before the Supreme Court of the United States, after moving through the lower courts for four years. As of this writing, the case is pending before the Court, and so we do not know what the outcome will be. The issue is an important one: Does freedom of the press, as guaranteed by the First Amendment, extend to high school newspapers? Or, do school principals have the right to censor high school newspapers? How did the United States Supreme Court decide? Your task is to find out. The decision will be announced late in 1987 or early in 1988.

There are many ways to learn what the decision was. How will you go about finding this information? Consult your school librarian, a reference librarian in your local library or a law librarian. Do you agree with the decision?

Case of the Censored School Paper

Detroit Free Press

•• DETROIT FREE PRESS/WEDNESDAY, OCTOBER 14, 1987 15A

School newspaper lawsuit weighs freedom of the press

By Bart Greenwald
Free Press Washington Staff

Sixteen-year-old Sue had it all—good looks, good grades, a loving family and a cute boyfriend. She also had a seven-pound baby boy.

WASHINGTON—The U.S. Supreme Court heard arguments Tuesday over the censorship of these words and others by a Missouri high school principal, in a case that could decide whether the First Amendment applies to about 20,000 high school newspapers across the country.

The hearing of Hazelwood School District vs. Cathy Kuhlmeier, which has been moving through the courts for four years, marks the first time the high court has been faced with the issue.

On behalf of the former students — Kuhlmeier, Lee Ann Tippett-West and Leslie Smart — St. Louis attorney Leslie Edwards said that Principal Robert Reynolds' censorship of the stories was improper because he was too removed from the classroom and his actions were based on his personal beliefs.

Edwards argued that the faculty adviser to the school newspaper should serve as editor, with the power to censor, "as long as it is not viewpoint-based."

Robert Baine Jr., the school district's attorney, told the court that the principal has the power to censor articles because it is a lab exercise and not a public forum for student views.

BUT PEOPLE involved with high school newspapers define the issue in much broader terms.

"The question is: Are (high school) student publications and (high school) students protected by the First Amendment?" Mark Goodman, executive director of the Student Press Law Center, said last week. "Are students going to be allowed to make their own content decisions, or are the schools going to be allowed to censor things they don't like?"

The Hazelwood stories which dealt with teenage pregnancy, marriage, runaways and the effects of parental divorce, were written for the Spectrum in 1983.

In 1984, in the case's first court test, a Missouri district judge ruled for the high school but was reversed last year by the U.S. Court of Appeals in St. Louis. The Supreme Court is expected to rule sometime next year.

Questions

1. Are there any reasons you can think of that make a high school paper different from other newspapers with regard to censorship?

2. Your local newspaper depends upon advertising to keep it afloat. It has to please many readers. A school newspaper does not need to please its readers or represent a majority view. School taxes keep the paper going. Does this affect your attitude toward freedom of the high school press?

3. Student journalists are not professionals and there is some question about whether they should be given the same consideration as professional journalists. What is your reaction to this statement?

4. How would the content of the school newspapers be affected if the principal had the final control over what was printed?

5. Do you believe that student journalists are responsible enough to choose stories to print without the need for censorship or guidance by teachers or principals? Explain.

6. Organize a debate around this statement: The First Amendment does not say ". . . except high school press . . . ." Therefore, freedom of the press should extend to school newspapers. See the First Amendment in the Appendix.

Activities

1. A concerned mother, Priscilla Prude, read an article about all of the bad things that can be found in *Mother Goose Rhymes*. Mrs. Prude was horrified to read the list of violent incidents which appear in the rhymes. She decided to organize a school council meeting to encourage nursery rhyme reform by cleaning up and pulling out nasty rhymes from the school library to protect the minds of little people.

   Read some *Mother Goose* rhymes and some *Grimm's Fairy Tales*. Organize the class into groups representing parents, teachers and librarians in the community. At this meeting take a position for or against Mrs. Prude's

plan to censor *Mother Goose*. Have specific examples from *Mother Goose* or *Grimm's Fairy Tales* which could be viewed as having a bad influence on little children.*

2. The third week of September is set aside by the American Library Association to observe "Banned Books Week." It is a reminder that censorship goes against the precepts of the Constitution and that the efforts to ban and censor books and otherwise stifle free expression are as vigorous as ever. We are reminded that the Holy Bible is the most banned and burned book in history. Challenges and demands for censorship come from many sources, especially those who are very concerned about young people.

Over the years, books of all kinds have been the target of people who want to censor reading material. These groups have different interests and different points of view. The motivation may be political, religious, educational or ethnic. Some may be concerned about ageist, racist and sexist literature.

To obtain a list of banned books or challenges which have occurred against books in the U.S., ask your school or public librarian, or write to: Director of the Office for Intellectual Freedom of the American Library Association, 50 East Huron St., Chicago, Illinois 60611, (312) 944-6780.

*See *Fact, Fantasy and Folklore*, by Lipson and Morrison, Good Apple, Inc., Carthage, Illinois, 1977, and *The Annotated Mother Goose,* by William S. Baring-Gould and Ceil Baring-Gould, the World Publishing Co., New York, 1962.

3. Try this: "Decisions About Censorship." Organize groups in class for the purpose of defining the word *censorship*. Students may use a dictionary to help. Each group will discuss and produce a written definition of *censorship* in their own words to be read aloud. Ask for questions after each reading. All the students are to listen carefully and take notes. Is there anything that is troublesome to anyone about each definition as it is read? (Experience bears out that two questions arise consistently: *Who* will do the censoring for all of us and *what* material will be censored or forbidden?) In an open, democratic society there are diverse points of view and no unanimous agreement on issues—educational or otherwise.

4. Some books censored have included: *Huckleberry Finn*, by Mark Twain; Anne Frank's *Diary of a Young Girl*; *In the Night Kitchen*, by Maurice Sendak (a picture book for children); *Making It with Mademoiselle* (a pattern book for dressmaking students published by *Mademoiselle* magazine); *The Autobiography of Ben Franklin*; *To Kill a Mockingbird*, by Harper Lee; *Animal Farm*, by George Orwell; *Great Expectations*, by Charles Dickens; *King Lear*, by Shakespeare; *The Red Badge of Courage*, by Stephen Crane; *A Separate Peace*, by John Knowles; and *Little Black Sambo*. Interestingly, *Fahrenheit 451*, the classic book by Ray Bradbury, which has also been censored, is an allegory about book banning in a repressive society. The title refers to the temperature at which paper ignites and burns. Ask your librarian how "Banned Books Week" is observed in your school library.

Glossary

A

Abate,
(verb) To end, terminate. As: to abate a nuisance.

Abridge,
(verb) To lessen or restrict. As: to abridge constitutional rights.

Abuse,
(noun) Improper or unlawful use of authority. Abuse may be physical, mental or procedural. A parent may be guilty of child abuse. A judge may be guilty of abuse of discretion. Child abuse is a criminal offense. Abuse of discretion by a judge may be reversible error in a trial.

Acceptance,
(noun) In contract law, the formal response to an offer to enter into a contract which, when received by the offeror, creates the contract.

Accuse,
(verb) To charge with a crime.

Acquit,
(verb) To find a person innocent of a crime after a trial. To find an accused person to be not guilty. As: he was acquitted by the jury.

Admissible Evidence,
(noun) Facts, testimony, or objects legally usable to prove a case in court.

Admission,
(noun) A statement by a party acknowledging their guilt or responsibility in a civil or criminal case.

Adopt,
(verb) To legally assume the role of a parent. To legally bring a person into a family.

Adversary,
(noun) An opponent.

Advocate,
(verb) To publicly support or argue for a cause or person. (noun) A person who advocates. A lawyer is an advocate.

Affidavit,
(noun) A written statement which the maker swears is true.

Affirm,
(verb) To confirm or support. As: an appeals court may affirm the decision of a lower court. (See Appeal.)

Affirmative Action,
(noun) The remedy used to correct past discrimination in hiring or promoting employees based on race and sex.

Age of Majority,
(noun) The age at which one becomes a legal adult. (See Majority.)

Agent,
(noun) A person or employee authorized to act in one's behalf.

Alias,
(noun) Meaning, "also known as." An assumed name.

Alibi,
(noun) A defense to a crime in which the defendant claims to have been somewhere else when the crime was committed.

Allege,
(verb) To assert a fact that one claims is true.

Allegation,
(noun) An assertion or charge.

Amendment,
(noun) An addition, correction, deletion, or improvement in a legal document.

Answer,
(noun) A formal response to a lawsuit or criminal charge.

Appeal,	(noun) The request made to a higher court to reverse the decision of a lower court. (See Grounds for Appeal.)
Appeals Court,	(noun) Also known as Appellate Court. A court designated to review the decisions made by lower courts when those decisions are appealed by a party. An appeals court will either affirm (uphold) or reverse (overrule) the decision of the lower court.
Arrearage,	(noun) Money owed and past due. As: there was an arrearage due.
Arrears,	(noun) The condition of owing an unpaid and overdue debt. As: he was $100.00 in arrears.
Arrest,	(verb) To deprive a person of his liberty by legal authority. To take a person into custody.
Assault,	(noun) An unlawful attempt or threat to strike another person. An attempted battery.
Attempt,	(noun) An act in pursuit of a crime which falls short of completing the crime.
Attorney,	(noun) A person given legal authority to act in another person's behalf.

B

Bail,	(noun) Money or other refundable security posted to insure that a defendant will appear in court at a later time. Judges usually set the amount of bail. (See the Eighth Amendment, Appendix. See also Bond.)
Bailiff,	(noun) An officer of the court who keeps order and helps carry out a judge's orders.
Battery,	(noun) An unlawful touching which harms or hurts another.
Bench,	(noun) The place where the trial judge sits. As: "Approach the bench." The collective name for members of the judicial branch of government.
Bench Warrant,	(noun) An arrest warrant ordered by a judge, issued for violating a court order.
Beyond a Reasonable Doubt,	(adverb) the standard of proof necessary to convict a criminal defendant. A very high standard requiring a moral certainty of the guilt of the defendant.
Bill,	(noun) A legislative proposal submitted for approval. In business, a request for payment. In law, a written request or order.
Bill of Rights,	(noun) The first ten amendments to the United States Constitution.
Bond,	(noun) Security posted for bail or for a debt. (See Bail.)
Boycott,	(noun) A group effort to halt commercial dealing.
Breach,	(verb) To fail to perform as promised or required. To break. As: "to breach a contract," or "to breach a duty."

Burden of Proof,	(noun) The level of proof necessary to win a lawsuit or criminal case. In criminal cases, the Prosecution has the burden of proof. In civil cases, the Plaintiff has the burden of proof.
Breaking and Entering,	(verb) To enter unlawfully into the premises of another with intent to commit a crime.
Burglary,	(noun) A breaking and entering into a dwelling at night to commit a crime.

C

Capital Offense,	(noun) A crime, such as murder or treason, punishable by death.
Capital Punishment,	(noun) Death penalty, for capital offenses.
Certiorari,	(noun) Certification granted when a court agrees to hear an appeal. As: The Supreme Court granted certiorari in a certain case.
Charge,	(noun), A criminal accusation or criminal complaint.
Circumstantial Evidence,	(noun) Indirect evidence.
Citation,	(noun) 1. A reference to a specific law or case, 2. A summons to court issued for violation of a law or statute.
Civil Infraction,	(noun) Violation of a civil law.
Civil Law,	(noun) Written laws concerning noncriminal legal matters.
Civil Rights,	(nouns) Rights granted by law to all people, to promote human dignity and social order.
Common Law,	(noun) Principles of law passed from one court to another on a case by case basis, building on precedent.
Compelling State Interest,	(noun), The overriding governmental necessity which must exist before the government is allowed to regulate or limit Fundamental Rights. (See Fundamental Rights.)
Compensation,	(noun) Money paid 1. for services performed, 2. for damages caused, 3. for property taken.
Complainant,	(noun) Plaintiff in a civil case or Complaining Witness in a criminal case. The complaining party.
Complaint,	(noun) A legal document alleging crimes committed or civil damages caused to the complainant by the defendant.
Condemnation,	(noun) A government act selecting property to take by eminent domain. (See Eminent Domain.)
Confess,	(verb) To admit guilt.
Conspiracy,	(noun) A criminal plan by two or more people, acting together.
Constitution,	(noun) The document that embodies the supreme laws and principles of an organization or country.
Contempt of Court,	(noun) Violation of a court order. Disobeying a judge or acting in a disrespectful way in court; punishable by fine or jail.

Contract,	(noun) A legally binding agreement between parties for goods or services.
Controlled Substance,	(noun) Any substance whose production, sale, or use is regulated by law.
Convict,	(verb) To find guilty of a crime. (noun) A person found guilty of a crime.
Copyright,	(noun) Exclusive rights granted by the government to artists, musicians and writers to control their works.
Corporal Punishment,	(noun) Physical punishment.
Counsel,	(verb) To advise. (noun) An advisor or lawyer.
Court,	(noun) The building or room where legal cases are conducted. Sometimes used to refer to the legal authority of the judge. As: a ruling of the court.
Court of Appeals,	(See Appeals Court.)
Crime,	(noun) An act which harms the public welfare and is made unlawful by a government.
Criminal,	(noun) A person who commits a crime, by an intentional or reckless act.
Cross-Examination,	(noun) Questions posed to a witness by an opposing attorney during a trial or deposition, following direct examination.
Custody,	(noun) A keeping or safeguarding. Control but not ownership.

D

Damages,	(noun) Legally recognized injuries. Monetary compensation paid for physical, emotional, or economic injuries or for breach of contract. As: the court awarded him $1000 in damages.
Deed,	(noun) A written document that transfers or conveys an interest in land.
Default,	(verb) To lose a lawsuit by failing to respond to a summons or complaint.
Defamation of Character,	(noun) The injury to a person's reputation caused by passing on false statements about that person.
Defendant,	(noun) One who must defend against a criminal complaint or defend against a civil lawsuit.
Defense,	(noun) A denial, explanation or answer to a criminal charge or civil lawsuit, denying responsibility or guilt.
Defraud,	(verb) To obtain something of value by fraud (by trick, lie, or misrepresentation).
Deposition,	(noun) An out-of-court statement by a witness made under oath in the presence of attorneys.
Direct Examination,	(noun) Questions asked to one's own witness during a deposition or trial.

Discretion,	(noun) The exercise of judicial power based on law, reason and experience. As: a judge must exercise but not abuse her discretion when sentencing a person convicted of a crime.
Dismiss,	(verb) 1. To deny a motion (request for action), 2. to end a lawsuit or criminal case before trial. A temporary dismissal is a "dismissal without prejudice." A permanent dismissal is called a "dismissal with prejudice."
Disorderly Conduct,	(noun) A crime involving loud, disturbing conduct such as fighting or public drunkenness. Also known as Disturbing the Peace.
Disturbing the Peace,	(noun) (See Disorderly Conduct.)
Divorce,	(verb) To legally dissolve a marriage with permission of the court.
Due Care,	(noun) The level of carefulness that people must exercise to avoid injuring others.
Due Process of Law,	(noun) A constitutional civil right granted by the Fifth and Fourteenth Amendments that requires a fair hearing before one can be punished.
Duty,	(noun) A legal obligation of one person to behave in a certain way to another.

E

Emancipation,	(verb) To free from bondage. Minors may be emancipated from their parents under some circumstances.
Eminent Domain,	(noun) The right of governments to purchase property for public use, even if the owner does not want to sell. (See Condemnation.)
Equal Protection of the Law,	(noun) Constitutional guarantee of equal treatment under law for people of all races, sexes, religions, national origins, or incomes. A civil right stated in the Fourteenth Amendment.
Evidence,	(noun) (See Admissible Evidence.)
Error,	(noun) Mistakes made in court proceedings. May be either reversible or harmless.
Examination,	(noun) Questions posed to a witness by an attorney in a trial or deposition.
Exclusionary Rule,	(noun) A rule which bars or excludes from use in trial any evidence that is improperly discovered by illegal police conduct.
Ex Post Facto Laws,	(noun) Latin, "after the fact." Laws which are unconstitutional because they try to punish a person for behavior that was legal when it was done.
Extenuating Circumstances,	(noun) Facts which reduce the guilt or responsibility of a person or explain otherwise wrongful behavior.

F

Fact Finder,	(noun) The party responsible for deciding the facts in a trial. In a jury trial the jury is the finder of fact. In other cases it is a judge or referee.

Fair Use,	(noun) The exception to copyright laws which allows scholarly and educational use of copyrighted materials without permission, if the use is not for profit.
False Arrest,	(noun) An unlawful arrest. A civil tort and/or a criminal act.
False Imprisonment,	(noun) An unlawful detention or restraint of freedom. A civil tort and/or criminal act.
Federal Courts,	(noun) Courts which enforce laws of the Federal Government of United States (in contrast to state laws). Federal courts also decide cases which involve more than one state and cases where a person is challenging a state law on constitutional grounds.
Federalism,	(noun) The system of government, as in the United States, where powers are shared between the individual states and a central government.
Felony,	(noun) A serious criminal act, usually punishable by over one year in prison and/or fines. Called a High Misdemeanor in some states.
Finding,	(noun) A decision of fact or law by a court.
Fraud,	(noun) An act which damages another by lie, trick, or misrepresentation. May be a violation of criminal and/or civil law.
Frisk,	(verb) To pat down the outer clothes of a person in order to detect a gun or weapon.
Fundamental Rights,	(noun) Basic civil rights granted, recognized, or implied by the Constitution.

G

Grand Jury,	(noun) A group of citizens usually working with a government prosecuting attorney who review facts and decide whether to seek criminal prosecutions (*indictments,* pronounced in-dite-ments) against people suspected of criminal behavior.
Grounds,	(noun) The underlying cause or justification for a case.
Grounds for Appeal,	(noun) The reasons an appellant (person making the appeal) gives for requesting an appeal. Most common grounds for appeal are the following errors by the trial court: 1. improper jury instructions, 2. allowing improper evidence or testimony, 3. not allowing proper evidence or testimony, 4. remarks by the judge that prejudiced the jury, 5. misinterpreting the law, 6. discovery of important evidence that was not available at trial. (See Reversible Error, Appeal, Appeals Court.)
Guilty,	(adjective) Having committed a crime proven either by admission or determined by a judge or jury.

H

Harmless, Error,	(noun) Procedural or legal error made during trial which is not serious enough to require reversal by Appellate Court.
Hearing,	(noun) A proceeding to determine factual issues in which evidence is taken and a decision is rendered.

Hearsay,	(noun) Testimony in which one person tells what someone else said. Usually not admissible in evidence at trial because of its unreliable nature.
Homicide,	(noun) Any killing, whether lawful or unlawful, of one person by another.
Hung Jury,	(noun) A jury which is unable to reach a verdict because of disagreement among its members.

I

Indictment,	(noun, pronounced in-dite-ment) A written accusation endorsed by a grand jury, formally accusing a person of criminal wrongdoing, and specifying the crime with enough specificity to allow the accused to prepare a defense.
Infraction,	(noun) A violation of a law.
Injunction,	(noun) A court order which prohibits a party from doing a certain act. (See Party.) An injunction is designed to protect and prevent irreparable harm.
In Loco Parentis,	(noun) Latin. A person or institution acting "in place of a parent."
In Re,	Latin, "in the matter of."
Intent,	(noun) The state of mind which motivates and is necessary for a wrongful act to be criminal. Some crimes require "specific intent." Other crimes have a lower standard requiring only "general intent" as shown by reckless behavior.

J

Joy Ride,	(verb) To temporarily use a motor vehicle without the permission of the owner (a criminal infraction).
Judge,	(noun) A public official either appointed or elected who interprets laws and conducts trials. A legal official who hears and decides cases.
Judgment,	(noun) The ruling made by a judge or jury after a trial, in favor of one of the parties, and against the other(s).
Jurisdiction,	(noun) The authority to hear and decide a case.
Jurist,	(noun) A legal scholar or judge.
Juror,	(noun) A member of a jury.
Jury,	(noun) A group of citizens drawn from the community who hear and decide the facts of a trial and render a verdict based on the laws as told them by the judge.
Juvenile Court,	(noun) A special court for hearing cases involving minors.
Juvenile Delinquent,	(noun) A minor who has committed a criminal act.

K

Kidnapping,	(noun) The criminal act of carrying off a person unlawfully or against his will.

L

Larceny,	(noun) Theft. Taking the property of another with the intent to permanently deprive the owner of the use or possession of the property.
Law,	(noun) Rules of conduct determined by legislatures and interpreted by courts, intended to maintain order and benefit the public welfare.
Lawsuit,	(noun) A civil action filed in court by a plaintiff asking the court to award the plaintiff money damages or other relief as a remedy to compensate the plaintiff for injuries allegedly caused by the defendant.
Lawyer,	(noun) A person licensed to practice law.
Liable,	(adjective) Legally responsible.
Liability,	(noun) Responsibility; either criminal, civil, financial, or equitable. A legal duty to act or pay for damages. A debt, not an asset.
Libel,	(noun) A false or misleading publication which tends to harm a person's reputation. (See also Defamation of Character.)
Liberty,	(noun) The freedom of activity granted by the Constitution and limited by laws only when its exercise interferes with the rights of others.
License,	(noun) Officially granted permission to engage in a legally restricted activity.
Litigation,	(noun) Lawsuits; legal action in court.

M

Majority, Age of,	(noun) The age at which one becomes a legal adult, responsible for his or her own affairs, contracts, and obligations. Age at which a person becomes eligible to vote (eighteen years of age pursuant to the Twenty-sixth Amendment passed in 1972).
Malice,	(noun) The intent to cause harm to others without justification.
Manslaughter,	(noun) A criminal homicide caused by recklessness or criminal negligence. The killing of a person caused by the gross misconduct of another who engaged in an activity with unnecessarily high risk such as drunk driving.
Marriage,	(noun) A contract enforced by the state in which a man and woman agree to live as husband and wife.
Minor	(noun) A person who has not yet reached the age of majority or legal adulthood.
Miranda Warnings,	(noun) Warnings which must be given to criminal suspects after arrest advising them of their right to remain silent, and to consult an attorney. Named after Miranda vs. Arizona. (See p. 25.)

Misdemeanor,	(noun) A minor crime usually punishable by less than one year in jail and/or a fine. In some states, more serious crimes are called High Misdemeanors rather than felonies.
Motion,	(noun) A request to the court for an order, ruling, or judgment.
Murder,	(noun) Unlawful killing of another. First degree murder is committed intentionally, with malice and premeditation (planning). Second degree murder is done intentionally, with malice, but without premeditation. Penalties are more severe for first degree murder.

N

Negligence,	(noun) Carelessness. Breach of duty of care expected of reasonable people.
Notice,	(noun) Legal notification of a pending action. The law requires that a person be given notice of legal action started against them before the court can act.
Notary Public,	(noun) A person authorized by law to validate signatures.
Nuisance,	(noun) Anything which disturbs, annoys, or interferes with the rights of a property owner to peaceful enjoyment of his property. A tort created by noise, odor, vibration, smoke, etc.

O

Offer,	(noun) In contracts, a promise which invites acceptance, and if accepted creates an enforceable contract.
Opinion,	(noun) The reasons a court or judge gives for the decision in a case.
Order,	(noun) A command issued by a judge, having the force of law.
Ordinance,	(noun) A local law. As: a city ordinance.

P

Party,	(noun) A person directly involved in a lawsuit, either Plaintiff or Defendant.
Patent,	(noun) An exclusive right granted by the government to inventors to use, sell, manufacture, or license their invention for seventeen years.
Perjury,	(noun) The crime of making false statements under oath.
Per Se,	(adjective) Latin, "by itself." For example, "negligence per se" is an act which by law is defined as negligent in and of itself.
Plagiarism,	(noun) The act of claiming the work of another as one's own.
Plaintiff,	(noun) The party that brings a lawsuit against a defendant. (See also Complainant.)
Plead,	(verb) To make a legal answer or argument. As: to plead "guilty" or "not guilty."

Police Power,	(noun) The constitutional authority granted to government to make and enforce regulations and laws reasonably related to protection of public health and safety.
Power of Attorney,	(noun) The appointment of a person to act in one's behalf.
Precedent,	(noun) A previously decided case used as authority in later cases on a similar subject. Courts must follow precedents set by higher courts.
Premeditation,	(noun) Forethought or planning. Used in reference to murder.
Preponderance of the Evidence,	(noun) The standard of proof required to win most civil cases (obtain a judgment). To prove a case, one must have the scales of justice tip at least slightly in one's favor.
Proximate Cause,	(noun) Direct or actual cause.
Prima Facie,	(adjective) Latin, "on first view," or "on its face." The basic showing of proof to make a case.
Probable Cause,	(noun) The basic constitutional requirement before a judge may issue a search warrant or arrest warrant. Also required before a police officer may arrest and search a suspect without a warrant. The officer or judge must have probable cause to believe that a crime has been committed and that the suspect committed it. (See the Fourth Amendment, Appendix.)
Probation,	(noun) Conditions set by a judge as an alternative to sending a convict to jail.
Proof,	(noun) Evidence required to establish or prove an allegation.
Prosecute,	(verb) To pursue a lawsuit or, more commonly, to seek a criminal conviction.
Prosecutor,	(noun) Also Prosecuting Attorney or District Attorney. The public official whose job is to prosecute those accused of crimes. Prosecutors must use their discretion to determine which acts are crimes and when there is enough evidence to charge a person with a crime.
Public Domain,	(noun) Public property, owned by all equally. As opposed to private property.

Q

Quid Pro Quo,	(noun) Latin, "something for something." The exchange of things of value in a contract.
Quiet Enjoyment,	(noun) The right of a property owner to undisturbed use of his lands.

R

Reasonable Doubt,	(noun) (See Beyond a Reasonable Doubt.)

Reasonableness,	(noun) A legal standard which assumes an average amount of intelligence and care.
Reasonable Person,	(noun) A legal standard which assumes that a reasonable person will behave in a reasonable manner. Juries are allowed to decide how a reasonable person would act in a given situation and judge a party to a lawsuit accordingly. Negligence is often defined as a breach of the duty of care that would be expected from a reasonable person.
Recess,	(noun) A temporary adjournment or break in a trial.
Reckless,	(adjective) Grossly negligent, heedless, willful and wanton. Conscious disregard of serious risk. More serious misconduct than ordinary negligence.
Relevant,	(adjective) Appropriate to prove a matter before the court. Evidence must be relevant to be admissible.
Remedy,	(noun) The means that a court uses to right the wrongs done to a plaintiff who proves his case. Money is the most common remedy awarded. Injunctions are granted to stop further wrongs from occurring in cases where money alone will not provide an "adequate remedy at law."
Resisting Arrest,	(noun) The crime of attempting to physically stop a lawful arrest.
Restitution,	(noun) Compensation for monetary loss.
Restraining Order,	(noun) A temporary injunction ordering a halt to some action until there is a complete hearing. Designed to stop irreparable damage that may occur before a full hearing, such as chopping down trees or tearing down a building.
Reverse,	(verb) To overturn or overrule. As: an appeals court may reverse the decision of a trial court.
Reversible Error,	(noun) An error committed during a trial that is so serious as to require a reversal of the court's ruling or verdict. (See Error and Appeal.)
Robbery,	(noun) Larceny from a person by force or threat of force.

S

Search Warrant,	(noun) A court order required by the Fourth Amendment, before police can enter and search a home or a person. It must specify the place to be searched and specific objects sought and cannot be issued unless the judge is convinced that there is probable cause. (See Probable Cause.) The requirement is designed to prohibit unreasonable searches and seizures by police or government officials.
Self-Defense,	(noun) The right to protect oneself or others from imminent attack. To be a valid defense to a charge of assault and battery, the force used must not exceed the amount necessary to repel the attack; the person using it must not be guilty of provoking or starting the fight; and in some states there must have been no opportunity to retreat easily to a place of safety.

Segregation,	(noun) Physical separation of people.
Sentence,	(noun) The punishment ordered by a court for one convicted of a crime. It may consist of fine and/or imprisonment, restitution to the victim, or probation.
Settlement,	(noun) An agreement between the parties to resolve a lawsuit before trial.
Shoplifting,	(noun) The crime of larceny (theft) of merchandise from a store.
Slander,	(noun) A false oral statement which defames or harms a person's reputation. (See Libel and Defamation of Character.)
Standard,	(noun) Criterion.
State Courts,	(noun) Courts which administer the laws of a state.
Statute,	(noun) A law passed by a legislature.
Statute of Limitations,	(noun) The law that limits the time in which a suit can be filed after a cause for a lawsuit or a criminal act occurs.
Subpoena,	(noun) An order to a witness to appear before the court, issued by a judge or court officer.
Summons,	(noun) A court order requiring a party to appear in court.
Sue,	(verb) To file a civil lawsuit in court.
Suit,	(noun) (See Lawsuit.)
Supreme Court,	(noun) The highest court of a state or of the United States.
Suspect,	(noun) A person suspected of, but not yet charged with, committing a crime.

T

Testimony,	(noun) Statements made in court, under oath, by a witness, and used as evidence.
Tort,	(noun) French, "wrong." An injury to a plaintiff directly caused by a breach of duty or care by a defendant, for which the court can award compensation to be paid by the defendant to the plaintiff, in an attempt to right the wrong.
Tort-Feasor,	(noun) French, "wrong-doer."
Trademark,	(noun) A word, symbol, or brand name used to identify and distinguish one product from another.
Trespass,	(noun) A wrongful interference with or invasion of the property of another.
Trial,	(noun) The conduct of a civil lawsuit or criminal proceeding in which blame or guilt is determined in a criminal action.
Truancy,	(noun) The unlawful absence from school.

U

Unconstitutional,	(adjective) An act or law which violates the Constitution and is therefore void and unlawful.

V

Valid,	(adjective) Legal, lawful and proper.
Verdict,	(noun) The final decision of a judge or jury in a civil lawsuit or criminal trial.
Void,	(adjective) Having no legal force. As if it never existed.
Void for Vagueness,	(adjective) A criminal law is void and unconstitutional if it is so vague that a reasonable person would not know what the law made illegal.
Voir Dire,	(noun) French, "to speak the truth." Examination of prospective jurors or witnesses to see if they are qualified, unbiased and truthful.

W

Warrant,	(noun) A written authorization issued by a judge.
Will,	(noun) A legal document which a person writes before his death indicating how he desires to have his possessions distributed after he dies.
Witness,	(noun) One who testifies in court, under oath, to facts he knows or events which he personally saw. Also a person who watches as someone signs an official document and so swears.

Appendix
The Constitution of the United States
Preamble

We the people of the United States, in order to form a more perfect Union, establish justice, insure domestic tranquility, provide for the common defense, promote the general welfare, and secure the blessings of liberty to ourselves and our posterity, do ordain and establish this Constitution for the United States of America.

AMENDMENT 1, 1791
Freedom of Religion, Speech, and the Press; Rights of Assembly and Petition

Congress shall make no law respecting an establishment of religion, or prohibiting the free exercise thereof; or abridging the freedom of speech, or of the press; or the right of the people peaceably to assemble, and to petition the government for a redress of grievances.

AMENDMENT 2, 1791
Right to Bear Arms

A well-regulated militia, being necessary to the security of a free state, the right of the people to keep and bear arms shall not be infringed.

AMENDMENT 3, 1791
Housing of Soldiers

No soldier shall, in time of peace be quartered in any house, without the consent of the owner, nor in time of war, but in a manner to be prescribed by law.

AMENDMENT 4, 1791
Search and Arrest Warrants

The right of the people to be secure in their persons, houses, papers, and effects, against unreasonable searches and seizures, shall not be violated, and no warrants shall issue, but upon probable cause, supported by oath or affirmation, and particularly describing the place to be searched, and the persons or things to be seized.

AMENDMENT 5, 1791
Rights in Criminal Cases

No person shall be held to answer for a capital, or otherwise infamous crime, unless on a presentment or indictment of a grand jury, except in cases arising in the land or naval forces, or in the militia, when in actual service in time of war or public danger; nor shall any person be subject for the same offense to be twice put in jeopardy of life or limb; nor shall be compelled in any criminal case to be a witness against himself, nor be deprived of life, liberty, or property, without due process of law; nor shall private property be taken for public use, without just compensation.

AMENDMENT 6, 1791
Rights to a Fair Trial

In all criminal prosecutions, the accused shall enjoy the right to a speedy and public trial, by an impartial jury of the state and district wherein the crime shall have been committed, which district shall have been previously ascertained by law, and to be informed of the nature and cause of the accusation; to be confronted with the witnesses against him; to have compulsory process for obtaining witnesses in his favor, and to have the assistance of counsel for his defense.

AMENDMENT 7, 1791
Rights in Civil Cases

In suits at common law, where the value in controversy shall exceed twenty dollars, the right of trial by jury shall be preserved, and no fact tried by a jury, shall be otherwise re-examined in any court of the United States, than according to the rules of the common law.

AMENDMENT 8, 1791
Bails, Fines, and Punishments

Excessive bail shall not be required, nor excessive fines imposed, nor cruel and unusual punishments inflicted.

AMENDMENT 9, 1791
Rights Retained by the People

The enumeration in the Constitution, of certain rights, shall not be construed to deny or disparage others retained by the people.

Amendment 10, 1791
Powers Retained by the States and the People

The powers not delegated to the United States by the Constitution, nor prohibited by it to the states, are reserved to the states respectively, or to the people.

AMENDMENT 13, 1865
Abolition of Slavery

Section 1. Neither slavery nor involuntary servitude, except as a punishment for crime whereof the party shall have been duly convicted, shall exist within the United States, or any place subject to their jurisdiction.

AMENDMENT 14, 1868
Civil Rights

Section 1. All persons born or naturalized in the United States, and subject to the jurisdiction thereof, are citizens of the United States and of the state wherein they reside. No state shall make or enforce any law which shall abridge the privileges or immunities of citizens of the United States; nor shall any state deprive any person of life, liberty, or property, without due process of law; nor deny to any person within its jurisdiction the equal protection of the laws.

AMENDMENT 15, 1870
Negro Suffrage

Section 1. The right of citizens of the United States to vote shall not be denied or abridged by the United States or by any state on account of race, color, or previous condition of servitude.

AMENDMENT 19, 1920
Woman Suffrage

Section 1. The right of citizens of the United States to vote shall not be denied or abridged by the United States or by any state on account of sex.

AMENDMENT 26, 1971
Suffrage for 18-Year-Olds

Section 1. The right of citizens of the United States, who are eighteen years of age or older, to vote shall not be denied or abridged by the United States or by any state on account of age.

Bibliography

Appenzeller, Herb, et al. *Sports and Law.* St. Paul, New York, Los Angeles, San Francisco: West Publishing Co., 1984.

Atkinson, Linda. *Your Legal Rights.* New York: Franklin Watts, 1982.

Bailey, F. Lee, and Rothblatt, Henry B. *Handling Juvenile Delinquency Cases.* Rochester, New York: Lawyers' Cooperative Publishing Co., 1982.

Baring-Gould, William S., and Baring-Gould, Ceil. *The Annotated Mother Goose.* New York: World Publishing Co., 1962.

Burton, William C. *Legal Thesaurus.* New York: MacMillan Publishing Co., Inc., 1980.

Carroll, Sidney B. *You Be the Judge.* New York: Lothrop, Lee and Shepard Co., 1971.

Family Legal Guide, A Complete Encyclopedia of Law for the Layman. Pleasantville, New York: The Readers' Digest Association, Inc., 1981.

Fincher, E. B. *The American Legal System.* New York, London, Toronto, Sydney: Franklin Watts, 1985.

Furlong, Mary S., and McMahon, Edward T. *Family Law.* St. Paul, New York, Los Angeles, San Francisco: West Publishing Co., 1984.

Gardner, Richard A. *The Boys and Girls Book About Divorce.* New York: Jason Aranson Publishers, 1983.

Gifis, Steven H. *Law Dictionary.* Woodbury, New York: Barron's Educational Series, Inc., 1975.

Gilbert, Michael, ed. *The Oxford Book of Legal Anecdotes.* New York: Oxford University Press, 1986.

Guggenheim, Martin. *The Rights of Young People.* Bantam, New York: American Civil Liberties Union, 1985.

Harnett, Bertram. *Law, Lawyers, and Laymen: Making Sense of the American Legal System.* New York: Harcourt, Brace Jovanovich, 1984.

Horowitz and Davidson, ed. *Legal Rights of Children.* New York: Shepard's McGraw Hill, 1984.

Johnson, Joan. *Justice.* New York, London, Toronto, Sydney: Franklin Watts, 1985.

Junior Scholastic: Who Makes the Laws?, Special Issue: U.S. Affairs Annual. Vol. 88, No. 10, Jan. 24, 1986.

Lipson, Greta, and Morrison, Baxter. *Fact, Fantasy and Folklore.* Carthage, Illinois: Good Apple, Inc., 1977.

Lockhart, W., Kamisar, Y., Choper, J. *Constitutional Rights and Liberties.* St. Paul, New York, Los Angeles, San Francisco: West Publishing Co., 1980.

McKown, Robin. *Seven Famous Trials in History.* New York: The Vanguard Press, Inc., 1963.

Olney, Ross R., and Patricia J., *Up Against the Law.* New York: E. P. Dutton, 1985.

Read, J., and Yapp, M. *Law.* St. Paul: Greenhaven Press, Inc., 1980.

Riekes-Ackerly. *Juvenile Problems and Law.* St. Paul, New York, Los Angeles, San Francisco: West Publishing Co., 1980.

Rofes, Eric, ed. *The Kids Book of Divorce: By, for & About Kids.* New York: Vintage Books, 1982.

Ross, Martin Jr., and Ross, Jeffrey Steven. *Handbook of Everyday Law,* Fourth Edition. New York: Harper & Row, 1981.

Sandburg, Don. *The Legal Guide to Mother Goose.* Los Angeles: Price/Stern/Sloan, 1981.

Stein, R. Conrad. *The Story of the Nineteenth Amendment.* Chicago: Children's Press, 1982.

Swiger, Elinor Porter. *The Law and You: A Handbook for Young People.* Indianapolis, New York: The Bobbs-Merrill Co., Inc., 1973.

Weinerman, Chester S. *Practical Law: A Layperson's Handbook.* Englewood Cliffs, New Jersey: Prentice-Hall, Inc., 1978.

Wolff, Robert, ed. *The Rule of Law.* New York: Simon and Schuster, 1971.